When they were young

WHEN THEY WERE YOUNG

Seventy celebrities recall their childhood

In aid of CLIC

the children's cancer trust

REDCLIFFE

Bristol

First published in 1990
by Redcliffe Press Ltd.,
49 Park St., Bristol

ISBN 1 872971 65 2

Designed by Ad Art Design, Bristol.
Typeset by Alphaset Creative Typesetting, Bristol.
Printed by Longdunn Press Ltd, Bristol.

British Library Cataloguing in Publication Data
When they were young: 70 celebrities recall their childhood
in aid of CLIC, the Children's Cancer Charity.
1. Celebrities – Biographies – Collections
I. Bladon, Richard
920.02

CONTENTS

FOREWORD

Her Royal Highness The Duchess of Kent, GCVO

Children who suffer from cancer or leukaemia show great courage in their fight against these diseases, often having to cope with years of painful treatment, hospitalization and separation from their families and loved ones. The CLIC Trust provides enormous support not only to the young patients but also to their families.

The proceeds from the sale of this book will be used to continue 'the fight to save young lives' and the Trust is most grateful to you for your support.

Patron

INTRODUCTION

The Cancer and Leukaemia in Childhood Trust has worked since 1976 to ensure that children with cancer receive the best possible treatment, that they and their families have welfare services available to them and that research into childhood cancer is funded. CLIC now has nineteen branches and their tremendous fund-raising activities have resulted in more than £5 million being raised so far. Publication of this book will give these funds a further valuable boost. The money will be well used.

The need to set up a charity became apparent to me in 1974 following the diagnosis of my son, Robert, to have a neuroblastoma tumour.

From its humble beginnings CLIC has achieved a great deal. CLIC House provides accommodation for up to forty people in a home-from-home environment whilst their children are receiving treatment. CLIC Annexe is an extension of CLIC House and provides overspill accommodation for a further ten people. CLIC Lodge in Plymouth, provides similar facilities for those attending Freedom Fields Hospital. CLIC Court is operated in tandem with CLIC Lodge and provides accommodation for those attending Derriford Hospital in Plymouth. CLIC Cottage caters for parents and their children attending the neurosurgery unit at Frenchay Hospital, in Bristol. CLIC 'crisis-break' flats are located at Sidmouth, East Devon and at Weston-super-Mare to give a much needed break to families at times of particular stress. With all these properties CLIC ensures that the whole family is catered for in an effort to keep it together at the most devastating time in their lives.

A team of domiciliary care nurses, also supported by CLIC, are attached to the various oncology clinics in Gloucester, Bristol, Bath, Taunton, Yeovil, Barnstaple, Torbay, Exeter, Plymouth and Truro. CLIC also funds a small team of playtherapists to help the young patients throughout their long stays in hospital. The Paediatric Oncology Unit at the Gloucester Royal Hospital and the extension to the Mother and Baby Unit at Bristol Children's Hospital were also funded by CLIC, and the Children's Cancer Unit which is located at the Bristol Royal Hospital and for which CLIC was mainly responsible, provides a regional service for the whole of the South West and has now treated more than 1,300 children.

The success of the Trust is perhaps best summed up by the fact that CLIC SW has been invited to present itself as a model of care for the whole of the United Kingdom. It is apparent that the excellence of overall care for parents and families makes CLIC unique, and a new, separate charity, to be named CLIC UK, will be launched during 1990. A number of invitations have already been received for the launch of CLIC Euro and the idea of CLIC Worldwide has also been suggested. It has been something of a shock to find that there is no similar organisation anywhere in this country, nor indeed in Europe, in fact one has yet to be found anywhere else in the world.

May I, on behalf of everyone involved in the CLIC Trust, express sincerest thanks to the many eminent people who have written for this book, to Richard Bladon who had the idea and researched the project, to the law firm of Lawrence Tucketts whose ready sponsorship turned an idea into reality; to the various publishers who have allowed us to use extracts from earlier books; to Quentin Blake who willingly contributed one of his inimitable cover designs for "When they were young" – and to you, the readers, who have helped our cause by buying this anthology. We are indebted to you all.

CLIC is indeed unique, and it is imperative that the same level of help and support given to young patients and their families in the South West of England is made available in every region of the country. The aim of CLIC is to change the world, the world of the child with cancer. It is my privilege to be the chairman of such a splendid, caring organisation and I look forward to the many new challenges of the 1990s with tremendous confidence that with your help CLIC will continue the fight to save young lives.

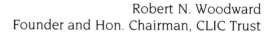

Robert N. Woodward
Founder and Hon. Chairman, CLIC Trust

JOHN LE CARRÉ
Author

Church Mice and Dorky Birds

When I was a small child, I had a number of misconceptions about The Almighty, and they tend to linger.

I thought Him overfond of mice, because I prayed to Him to pity mice implicitly. I know now that I was asking for divine indulgence for my own simplicity, but the misconception dies hard.

I thought it better to be a dorky bird in the house of the Lord than to dwell in the courts of iniquity. I still do, but I know now that the reference was to doorkeepers, though the dorky bird, with its image of spread wings and effortless levitation, and its affectionate waddle, still seems to me a far better thing to be.

Years later, when I was in the Foreign Service, I confessed my misconceptions to a grand bishop, who was visiting our embassy abroad. He was greatly shocked that my prayers should, so to speak, have got into the wrong stream of traffic.

Never mind, I'm sure God had a jolly good laugh all the same.

FRANKIE HOWERD OBE

Actor and comedian

Struck Dramatically

As far back as I can remember, I seemed to be stage-struck one way or another. I loved going to the pictures and pantomime, listening to the radio, putting on little shows at the bottom of our garden — dressed in some of our parents' clothes, which we borrowed when they weren't looking. I made my first stage appearance when I was thirteen in the Church Dramatic Society where they made me up to look middle-aged, with the help of a beard and grey wig, and I played the part of the father of a lady who was old enough to be my mother. The church warden told me then that I was going to be an actor and I thought this was the voice of God speaking, and so I was determined to carry out His wishes and become a dramatic actor. It seems that either I or the church warden got God's message wrong since I ended up as a music-hall clown. Nevertheless, I thank God I did!

SUE LAWLEY

Broadcaster

But not with a Heart of Stone

 hen I was sixteen, I was asked to play the part of Hermione in a school production of *The Winter's Tale* by William Shakespeare. Those of you who know the play will remember that Hermione, wrongly accused of infidelity by her jealous husband, Leontes, is transformed into a statue. She only returns to life at the end of the play when Leontes repents.

For me, the greatest test of my abilities came not during the bits of the play where I spoke – I seemed to manage those all right – but in the long passage where I had to play a statue. As I recall, I was expected to stand on a rather wobbly platform while the rest of the cast marched around in a state of high emotion discussing death, grief, forgiveness and all sorts of other things as well. How was I, a chatty fifth former, to stand calm and immobile for at least a quarter of an hour in full public view?

Miss Ambrose had the answer. She was the headmistress and always took an interest in our youthful performances. 'Stare at one spot and one spot only, my dear,' she said. 'If your eyes aren't moving, your body won't either.'

On the opening night, I took Miss Ambrose's advice. Climbing gingerly onto the fragile set constructed with loving care, but shaky technique, by Mrs Blewitt, the history mistress and our domestic science teacher, Miss Fisher, I fixed my gaze on a point in the middle distance as the curtains opened and the last scene began.

Miss Ambrose, I discovered, was quite right. If your eyes didn't move, neither did your body. As my fellow pupils declaimed and gesticulated around me, I remained motionless. The perfect statue.

The moment came for me to come to life again. 'Music . . . awake her! Strike!' was my cue. Slowly, I turned my head to begin my descent onto the main part of the stage. As I did so, my eyes now released from their long concentrated gaze, suddenly filled with water. I raised my head to look my long lost husband in the eye and as I did so that water streamed down my face like tears!

Miss Ambrose, sitting in the front row, gasped. Never before had she seen one of her pupils so visibly moved by Shakespearian emotion. Here, she thought, was a girl of great sensitivity; could she not be an actress one day?

I never had the heart to tell her how I had managed to appear so moved that night on the stage in the school hall, and avoided her kindly enquiries as to whether I might pursue a career in the theatre. I knew that I had cried by accident, not by design. I did not have the talent to be such an actress, even though I was quietly thrilled to have made such an impression on the first night.

By the way, I failed to cry on the second night.

Father of the Man

The incidents of childhood are either dull or embarrassing. The school play was neither for the performers, but both for the audience. (I was very upset on one occasion when my parents thought young Daniel Massey a better actor than me.) My acting career at school had variety at first. Later it settled into a pattern – some say it has never stopped.

At the age of ten I played Doll Tearsheet in *Henry* IV *Part* 2; this was unsuitable, as I was one of few at that age whose voice had broken, and in any case, I did not understand what the lady was up to. I would have preferred to be the Lord Chief Justice – or at least Exeter in *Henry* V – and answer the question 'What treasure, uncle' with 'tennis balls, my liege.' The next year, I was Bolingbroke in *Richard* II – another rotten part. Who on earth, when faced with a deportation order, would believe that:

All places that the eye of heaven visits
Are to a wise man ports and happy havens?

At sixteen the producer of *Macbeth* (Timothy Renton) selected the three most disorderly boys in the school as First, Second and Third Murderers: Stephen Egerton (now KCMG), Neal Ascherson (*Independent on Sunday*) and myself. Unfortunately the props department thought that a squawk of the clarinet would do for 'the owl that shrieked' and the audience rocked with laughter. Besides Banquo, our instructions were to kill Fleance (Tam Dalyell); but Shakespeare let him escape.

Pomposity eventually prevailed in the next year, as Canon Chasuble in *The Importance of Being Earnest*, with Renton as Gwendolen. By the time that I was eighteen the die was cast, with two lawyers' parts on speech-day. The first was Cicero declaiming on self-defence in *Pro Milone*. It was marvellous stuff for a jury:

Non potestis hoc facinus improbum judicare, quin simul judicetis omnibus, qui in latrones inciderint, aut illorum telis aut vestris sententiis esse pereundum.

(If you convict my client, you will decide that everyone who is set upon by robbers must perish either by their weapons or by your verdict.)

The second was Sergeant Buzfuz in *Pickwick Papers* – a prolix, bombastic and unconvincing lawyer. So the child is father of the man.

DEBORAH KERR
Actress

Theatrical Things and Newts

 was an over-sensitive child and consequently was terribly bullied and teased by the other girls at school because they knew they could make me cry. Nice young girls, weren't they? I have a brother, Ted, who is four years younger than me, and, poor boy, I think I took out on him, at holiday times, the teasing and bullying I received at school.

I was always very keen on theatrical things and had a small theatre with curtains which functioned, and I made up the plays and drew the characters, which were pushed onto the stage by long strips of cardboard. I would play some of the parts, and demand that Ted play the others. If he forgot his lines or forgot to push on his characters I would be *furious*! Poor long suffering boy – I even used to dress him up in my mother's clothes and hats, and it is amazing he turned out to be such a very dear and normal person. But we had many good times – making mud pies and pretending we had a shop – and relatives would be asked to come and see our wares, and of course pay for them. We made quite a few pennies that way.

We lived in a cottage with a large meadow at the back, and Ted and I would go to the pond and catch newts, which I would then put in a fish bowl with small rocks and greenery – along with the goldfish I had once carried all the way home from boarding school in a jam jar with string around the top to serve as a handle. It's surprising that this poor fish survived at all, because by the time it had been transported from Bristol to my home on the Sussex-Surrey border there was hardly any water left in its jar. The newts we caught were a constant source of wonder, for they would shed their skins (out of terror, poor things, although we weren't to know that then) and leave a transparent replica of themselves in the fish bowl. I remember taking the skins back to school where they were of much interest in the biology classes.

I have many happy memories of my childhood. I was unhappy at boarding school, but my holidays at home in Alfold were a joy – even if they weren't for my brother Ted!

THE RT REV BARRY ROGERSON
Bishop of Bristol

The Half-Term Holiday

The smell of grease-paint and the taste of Marmite and sweet salad cream bring the memories flooding back. It could have only been three or four October half-term holidays but they brought a life-time of enjoyment.

I lived in Newark by the side of the Trent. My grandparents, with whom I spent the half-term holidays, lived in West Timperley, not far from Altrincham and Manchester. The journey meant catching a number of buses and changing in Nottingham and Buxton before being met in Manchester by my grandfather. The journey took most of the day and my mother ensured that I had sufficient to eat. Two sets of sandwiches, one for lunch and the other for tea. I knew that when we reached Buxton it was time for tea and the Marmite and sweet salad cream sandwiches were there to be enjoyed.

My grandfather was an accountant by profession, but in his spare time was a baritone who sang with local choirs and amateur operatic societies. Both he and my grandmother were involved in amateur dramatics and with the local repertory company. So it was hardly surprising that the few days I spent with them seemed to have been a constant whirl of visits to the theatre and the cinema.

Here was an entirely different world in which imagination and fantasy could enlarge the boundaries of a child's experience. When the lights went down in the cinema or the theatre the real world was banished and a new and exciting world of colour, sound and action took its place. The cinema at Hale was a regular venue for this new world. There with Sabu in the film *The Arabian Nights* I could join the acrobats and dancers as they helped the Caliph of Baghdad win back his throne. When the desert encampment was set on fire the heat of the flames drove me back in my seat. The darkness obliterated the boundaries between fantasy and reality.

The Garrick Theatre was the local rep. and here I was introduced to the plays of Ben Travers and the world of farce. Best of all was *Arsenic and Old Lace*. This black comedy blurred the boundaries between what was right and what was amusing. The theatre is never as dark as the cinema but when the character on stage is also your grandfather the boundaries between fantasy and reality were blurred even more.

My grandmother died while I was still at school and in her will she left me her make-up box. The smell of grease-paint brings back those years when I was given a love of the cinema and the theatre, a gift which is still enjoyed. This is hardly surprising because in every clergyman there is a Hamlet trying to get out!

BERNARD LEVIN CBE

Journalist and author

Gas-Lit Memories

hen the trigger that fires off memory is that of the most evocative of the senses, smell, my feats of memory astonish even me. There is one scent that I have not come across for many years now – not surprisingly, for it is that of a 'mantle', the glowing pipeclay lattice which surrounds a burning gas-jet to give light, and I have not been in a house lit by gas for a long time. But when my nose stumbles across a scent close enough to the gas mantle for it to unlock the same door (the striking of a safety match will do) the entire scene of my gaslit childhood home is reproduced in my mind's eye with such profusion of detail that I yearn for a magic camera that can photograph memories.

I have just struck the match, and the picture is before me as though I had walked into a darkened room and switched the light on. I can see the exact pattern, red and blue dentils, of the linoleum; the furniture, including the Windsor chairs which, the collective family memory has told me, I once beat all over with a hammer when my mother was out, so that they were ever afterwards pitted with dents; the heavy sideboard with its fringed 'runner', and the massive bronze pestle and mortar standing on it beside the samovar, these being the only physical possessions my maternal grandparents had brought with them on the long trek from the pogroms of late nineteenth-century Russia; the view from the window – not much of a view in those rows of back-to-backs; and, high up on the wall, the gas burning with a gentle sizzling sound in its little cage. (I have often promised myself that when I am a millionaire I shall have a room in my house lit by gas, regardless of expense – including, presumably, the cost of hiring a craftsman to reproduce the apparatus – just so that I can have the pleasurable smell whenever I want it. I also plan to be followed about the streets by a man pushing a hurdy-gurdy, which will play the hurdy-gurdy tune from *Petrushka* over and over again.)

There are never any human figures in the childhood scenes thus conjured into being by the appropriate scent, at any rate until I make a conscious effort to summon them up, though there is always a cat; indeed, nothing at all is actually happening, and certainly I can never see myself. But I can see very clearly the battered armchair in which I used to settle myself with a book, and find oblivion.

The cat is Tim, a handsome Persian of whom I have written elsewhere; he is the first cat I can remember, though not the first cat in my life, for there is another family story, from well before Tim, that on a hot summer's day with the windows open, in the room with the pitted chairs, I was whirling a towel round my head and caught the cat, sunning itself on the window sill, a glancing blow, causing it to fall three storeys to the ground. It survived the experience, I learned, but got into the habit of sitting on the stairs and spitting at me as I went past on my way to bed.

PATRICK MOORE CBE
Author

In the Dark!

re you afraid of the dark? I'm not sure if I ever was; if so, I overcame it at the age of six in a rather curious way.

I had picked up a book belonging to my mother, who was slightly interested in astronomy. I read it (it wasn't a boy's book, but my reading was all right), decided that this was interesting, and made up my mind to pursue it. I invested my 6d pocket money on a star map, and made a pious resolution to identify one new constellation every clear night. I then lived at East Grinstead, in Sussex; it was winter, so darkness fell by teatime.

I could hardly wait until dark. I obtained parental permission to stay up 'after hours', and then, when it was really dark, went outdoors. I suppose our garden covered about an acre. Looking up at the stars, I instantly recognized the Great Bear. Good start! What next? The Little Bear, the Dragon, or what?

It wasn't nearly so difficult as I'd expected, and within half an hour I had located several constellations with certainty. Then I heard a call from an upstairs window; time to go indoors. But where was the door? At my request, indoor lights had been turned off or screened. I was in pitch darkness, lost.

I remember a feeling of panic. Bogeys and things which went bump in the night . . . real or not? Then I looked up – there was the Bear – walk *this* way and I may find the tennis-net . . . I did. It took me about a quarter of an hour to get indoors, I think, but I had learned my lesson. Next day I spent my following week's pocket money on a torch, and never since then have I been known to move without one.

Which, considering how much of my life I've spent in the dark, is just as well!

Terry Hands

Gordon Honeycombe

Michael Winner

MICHAEL WINNER

Chairman, Scimitar Films Ltd

Traffic Lights and Search Lights

The first years of my life, some four in all, were lived in a small imitation mansion in Willesden. I remember the delights of looking out of the window at the lamplighter as he went on his bicycle lighting the gas lights in the street. A view of light in the dark has always intrigued me which is possibly why I went into cinema.

Later on we transferred to Lancaster Gate, near Paddington Station, where the traffic lights at the end of the road in blacked out, wartime London equally fascinated me. Those lights were added to on many nights by the excitement of bombs going off, and guns firing from the park nearby, searchlights and all the panoply of war which to a child of five was deeply entertaining! From there I was evacuated to a boarding school in Hertfordshire and like most Londoners the sight of woods and lakes and ponds was wondrous. How sad that today when you look at these beauties of nature your mind thinks about how polluted they are, how close they are to factories on the left or the right, or overhead to aeroplanes and acid rain. The innocence of looking at our planet has been clouded forever for future generations. That is surely one of the greatest sadnesses in the world today.

BRYAN FORBES
Writer, film director and producer

Tuppenny Rush

s a child I was an inveterate cinema goer, and in those days you got value for money. Most of my contemporaries patronized the 'Tuppenny Rush' at the Splendide alongside Forest Gate railway station. There, on a Saturday afternoon, we would rush the doors to tread the threadbare carpets inside that dark and welcoming cave. For thruppence you could join the ranks of the élite and sit upstairs in the balcony, a privilege which carried with it the bonus of being able to hurl your ice-cream carton on the unruly audience below. The programme was lavish. There were always two feature films, an episode of a serial, a cartoon, and a newsreel. Our favourite was Buster Crabbe in *The Vanishing Shadow*, but we cried with Rin Tin Tin, booed lustily if any of the cowboy heroes so much as held a girl's hand, and were constantly in a state of readiness to pelt the unfortunate manager when the equipment broke down. To this day I can recall the agonizing delight of those afternoons . . . but if the Splendide was my village church, the Queens at the top of Woodgrange Road was my Westminster Abbey. This superior palace, glorifying the Cunard-liner-style of British cinema architecture, demanded greater respect and the collection started at sixpence. It was there, on Friday nights, that blissful childhood day of the week when school can be pushed to the back of the mind, that I first became addicted. I saw Laurel and Hardy there, and Will Hay, Graham Moffat, Ernie Lottinga, Moore Marriot, Sonnie Hale and Jessie Matthews. Miss Matthews was my first screen crush and I included her in my prayers, asking God to keep her for me until I was of age. When I discovered that she was married to Sonnie Hale my sense of deprivation was acute. Claude Dampier was another favourite, and of course Cicely Courtneidge and Jack Hulbert; I was moved to tears by *Soldiers of the Queen*. With the exception of Laurel and Hardy, who in any event were exports to Hollywood, my affections were mostly confined to British stars. I recall that in the company of another friend I once went at opening time to see *Oh, Mr Porter*. We sat through three complete performances to emerge after dark into the irate arms of two distraught mothers and a policeman. We resorted to all manner of subterfuge, not to say dishonest practices, to gain our ends when the

fever ran highest and the kitty was empty. The simplest and most effective ploy at the poor old broken-down Splendide was to raise the money to buy one ticket. Once inside, the owner of the ticket would then work his way to the remotest exit, carefully open the door where his partners in crime would be waiting outside. They would dart in like rats and occupy the nearest vacant seats. The aged usherettes were too bored and poorly paid to give chase, but from time to time a new manager (pathetically attired in some second-hand dress suit) would brush the dandruff off his collar and attempt a purge. He didn't stand a chance, of course. Selected stooges would allow themselves to be captured and evicted whilst greater hordes, taking advantage of the planned diversion, would swarm through every orifice and occupy the house. Now, as a film producer, I cannot possibly condone such foul practices, but in those days it seemed a natural way of life.

ROSEMARY SUTCLIFF OBE, FRSL

Writer of historical novels

The Magic Christmas Tree

he first Christmas tree that I remember belongs to, I think, my sixth Christmas.

I know that I had had at any rate one Christmas tree before that, because my mother used to tell me how my father 'brought home a Christmas tree from the Admiralty' and decorated it for my first Christmas; but at eleven days old one does not remember much. By the time I was three, we were in Malta, following the Mediterranean Fleet; and the only trees I remember in Malta are branches of heavy golden oranges hanging over high walls from hidden gardens on the far side.

But by my sixth Christmas we were back in England, and 'home' had become a tall Georgian house in Sheerness Dockyard; and that Christmas we spent with my Uncle Harold and Aunt Kythé in Dorset.

We drove down on Christmas Eve, all three of us sitting in a row in the front seat of the family Morris Cowley, so my father must have been feeling poor just then, because for years we had Morris Cowleys or Morris Oxfords according to whether he was feeling poor or not-quite-so-poor at the time. It was cold and rather wet, and the rain came in even though we had the hood up; and I – my place was against the passenger door and consequently the passenger window – was cold and tired and damp and faintly tearful by the time we arrived. My mother shovelled me straight into bed with a cup of hot milk, and half an asprin to take care of my inability to sleep in strange beds. And I remember nothing more of that Christmas Eve.

But some while before, Aunt Kythé had asked me what I wanted for Christmas and I had said, not thinking about it very much, that I would like a Christmas tree with all its decorations on, and had then forgotten about it altogether. But when I woke on Christmas morning, the nobbly pillowcase of delights left for me in the night by Father Christmas had to await its turn, taking second place, because there, on a table at the foot of the bed, stood the first Christmas tree of my life, not counting the unremembered Admiralty one!

The light must have been on for I remember the tree's stick insect shadows pencilled on the wall behind it. It was an artificial tree, and so without the depth and density of the real thing – but I did not then know the real thing anyway – and I gazed speechless at the fantastical beauty before me, glimmering with tinsel, decked and magical with blown-glass baubles, tin-foil icicles and golden bells and silver stars, the gauzy fairy at the very top, the shiny coloured candles clipped to every spidery sharp-etched branch and my cup spilleth over.

I did not want to touch, only to look and look and look, my gaze lingering on one after another of the minuscule treasures, but returning again and again to one in particular. I have wondered, since, what made that one so special among all the rest; but after all, one does not love things or people for their special beauty or virtue, only for being themselves. This was a little yellow papier mâché bird with real yellow feathers for its wings and tail. This was different. This I must touch, my heart having gone out before me. I leaned over the foot of the bed, forefinger advanced and touched very gently; it bobbed and swung in answer to any touch, so that in some deep and secret place we were in communication with each other . . .

All the other treasures blur, when I try to remember them, into General Effect, into the shimmer and glow of the archetypal Christmas tree, but the little yellow bird I remember in every detail. I cherished him through many Christmases, until he ceased to be – worn out by old age or lost in one of the many house-moves of a sailor's family – but never forgotten.

For his sake I still look for a little yellow bird on counters of Christmas tree decorations (but have never found one worthy to take his place). For his sake I have bet on hopeless outsiders because they were called Yellowbird. For his sake a Dresden plate with a pale and slender canary on it hangs in my bedroom.

I am the richer for having known and loved him since that Christmas when I was six years old.

DUDLEY MOORE
Actor and composer

Singing for Mince Pies

 'm enclosing an early favourite photograph of myself, just to show what a petulant perverse creature I was!

My memories of childhood are mainly smoked out by now, but my fondest memories are of Christmas time, when I used to go around with the local church choir singing outside houses and being invited in for mince pies. The church always looked so extraordinarily festive and it was such a thrill for me as a young boy to play the organ at the church services or to sing in the choir. They were without doubt the most colourful and memorable days of my childhood. They remain with me as a pleasant and very beautiful dream. Incidents I don't seem to remember too much. Those I do, I prefer not to!

Dudley Moore

SIR NICHOLAS LYELL MP, QC
Solicitor General

Witness of Disaster

n 1944 I was five years old.

We lived at Chipperfield in Hertfordshire on the edge of the common and happily my memories of the war are limited. I remember seeing a barrage balloon when visiting my grandparents in London. I remember the blackout and the air raid warnings, but I am still unclear which warning was which, the wailing siren and the long steady blast which I think was the all-clear. I remember the chicken wire over the kitchen windows against bomb blast and once I recall that we all had to stand under the stairs when a doodlebug had strayed far off course into the vicinity. It was likely to crash at any moment but I do not recall its doing so.

One day we found the woods on the common full of strips of silver foil known as lattice. It was dropped by the German aeroplanes to try to confuse the radar. We used to collect it and we put it on our Christmas tree.

Our house was only two miles from the large American airfield at Bovingdon. I was an avid aeroplane spotter with charts showing the different types. My favourite was the fastest of all, the Lockheed Lightning, with its twin fuselage. I never saw a jet at that time.

Three incidents stand out in my mind; one historic, one disturbing and the last tragic and in slow motion.

One day I looked up to see the air full of aeroplanes. They were in serried ranks, one towing another. They were on their way to Arnhem.

The disturbing incident was just after dusk one evening. My father rushed outside very agitated. An aeroplane was buzzing the house. Apparently he waved and shouted at it to go away. But it turned and again flew low over the chimney pots. His shouts were in vain for we later heard that it had crashed two miles away and one of its engines had rolled into somebody's kitchen. The crew had bailed out hours before.

The final incident was on a summer's day. We were over with my father and mother by a neighbouring farm. I do not recall hearing anything but when I looked up I saw a large aeroplane in two parts. It was a four engined bomber. Its tail was falling backwards one way, its huge body beginning to fall forwards the other way. For a moment it hardly moved and then plunged downwards into the ground at the bottom of the field. My father covered my younger sister's eyes. A huge mass of flame and black smoke shot upwards.

The aeroplane had been a Flying Fortress. It had had eleven people on board including two nurses, we were told later. My father rushed down the field, no doubt to see if there was anything he could do but it was plain that no one could have survived. I never saw the other plane but apparently the bomber had been sliced in two by a twin engined monoplane. Miraculously that had not crashed at once and the two occupants had bailed out safely.

TERRY HANDS

Artistic Director, Royal Shakespeare Company

Looking after Teddy

 remember at night the sirens and the bombers and the shelter in the garden and Teddy who got frightened and needed a lot of looking after.

And I remember at dawn barefoot in pyjamas and home-made dressing gown looking for the strips of silver paper which fell in the night and crunching them into balls to give to the man who came once a week with horse and cart and took them away to buy guide dogs for the blind.

And I remember in the day the doodle-bugs and their sudden silence and Teddy having to sit under the table until the bump and the telling of 'The Story'.

Once upon a time the man next door was in the bath when the doodle-bug stopped grumbling and he grabbed his tin hat and ran down to get into the cupboard under the stairs but could only get half in because the rest of the family were there already and the front door was open because his wife had been outside and an air-raid warden looked in and saw him still pink and steamy with his head and shoulders only under the stairs and he said, 'Alf, if you are going to stay like that, you will need your helmet on the other end'. And we all laughed. Every time the doodle-bugs came we told the story. There seemed to be a lot of doodle-bugs.

And I remember VE Day and the long tables in the street and 'Knees-up Mother Brown' and 'One Finger One Thumb Keep Moving' and 'Hey Cokey Cokey Cokey' and the races and not falling over and winning a bar of very hard chocolate.

The war did seem a terribly complicated way of buying guide dogs or winning a bar of chocolate – even at the time.

SIR JOHN HARVEY-JONES MBE

Former chairman ICI, chairman Wildfowl and Wetlands Trust

The Perambulator Slalom

 n my experience childhood memories tend to be of the snapshot variety rather than a continuance of events.

My earliest such memory dates from a time when I was in a pram. We were staying with my grandparents who had retired from India and were living at the top of Lynton Bank in North Devon. My nursemaid at that time, but not for long thereafter, was taking me for my daily perambulation accompanied by a very small and short-legged black Scottish Terrier. At the top of the bank, which is of immense steepness, she let go of the pram which, with the Scottie in full pursuit bounced down the hill at ever increasing speed. My memories consist of watching the sky and clouds flash by the top of the pram to the accompaniment of banshee wails from the nursemaid and excited barks from the Scottie.

My introduction to the four-wheeled downhill perambulator slalom occurred when the pram tipped over at the first bend.

GORDON HONEYCOMBE

Author, playwright, dramatist, television presenter and narrator

Rigours of the Raj

 was born in Karachi, then in British India, in 1936. My father worked for an American oil company, and it was not until after the war that we returned to Scotland. Although we lived fairly ordinary lives in a large flat, this was India, and we had four servants. As a baby, I had an *ayah*, an Indian nanny. My earliest memory is of being in a pram and drowning in the heat. *Ayahs* took their charges out for an airing, and mine must have left me too long in the sun. Perhaps she had an assignation. More likely, she was chatting with some friends.

I nearly drowned for real when I was five or six. A breaker overwhelmed me as I paddled in the Indian Ocean. Dragged under, I disappeared. Only my sun-hat floating on the water signalled my whereabouts. Before this I nearly died when I was smitten at the same time by whooping cough and measles. I was very ill. I remember feeling very uncomfortable and feverish in a cot shrouded with a mosquito net. Another nasty experience was when I had my tonsils out. There was blood on the pillow afterwards and my throat was horribly sore. That wasn't all. I once had a stye under an eye-lid that had to be cauterized, and for a time I suffered from worms. As all children were regularly inoculated then against smallpox, chicken-pox, typhus and cholera, it's not surprising that I developed a dread of injections and needles (they were thicker then) and an aversion to doctors and hospitals. No. Growing up in India seldom guaranteed unfailing good health. In addition, I was a thin and anaemic child.

But I survived, and my childhood otherwise was sublimely untrammelled, happy and free. It was only when we returned to the shortages, damp and chill of postwar Britain, to bleak Auld Reekie (Edinburgh) that I swapped the medical rigours of the Raj for recurring rounds of colds, coughs, hay fever and flu. I'm all right now.

FREDERIC RAPHAEL
Author

The American Kid

he Jesuits, we are always told, have only to have a child for the first seven years of his life for them to be able to imprint their message upon him forever. There is no risk of my being marked (or saved) by their indoctrination. The first seven years of my life were spent (apart from brief sorties) in the United States. My transplantation to England was neither painful, nor by the standards of the century, more than mildly traumatic. My mother may have been American, but my father was British-born and, although a resident of the U.S. for some years, he had an unmistakable Oxford accent. It says something for his charm that he sold oil products to the Irish gas-station managers in Illinois without being accused of being an agent of King George V. (The king himself, on a visit to my 'home-town', Chicago, was less amiably received.)

My American mother was born in Kansas City but she had gone to work for an architect in Chicago, where she met my father. I was born at the Grant Hospital in 1931, when Al Capone had made the city notorious. A motorist, given a ticket for speeding, observed with accurate bitterness, 'You can't get away with anything in Chicago except murder.' You could, of course, but you had to know where to pay your subscription.

I spent only a few months in Chicago, before my parents went to live in St Louis. My passport reminds me of a place I could scarcely claim to recall. Yet, when I have visited the windy city (its chill factor, in the winter months, gives it an Arctic severity), I have a fatuous sense of belonging, if not of proprietary rights. The mention of State Street ('That great street', as the songs insists) and of the Edgewater Beach Hotel – where my parents danced – and of the 'South Side' and the 'Loop' – the business district where the overhead railroad takes a slowing bend right in front of the skyline which Louis Sullivan and Frank Lloyd Wright helped to create, the unmistakable skyscraping profile of the quintessential American city, evokes in me that lumpish emotion which, however irrational, reminds me that, for all my half-century of English and European attachment, I was – and, to an undeniable degree, remain – an American kid.

My childhood coincided with the best and the worst of American times. Do I really remember the lines outside the soup kitchens when, in 1935, we drove from Aurora, Illinois, through Columbus, Ohio, (in a jalopy with an external 'rumble-seat' in which my grandmother travelled – Americans would say 'traveled' – uncomplainingly)? I think I do. My father was on his way to a new, better job in Shell Oil, but many Americans (although FDR had been president for three years) were desperate and unemployed. Yet – outside Chi, at least – it seemed a time of order; you could walk without hesitation across Central Park at night. I used my scooter there, among the red squirrels which are now, I fear, all but extinct, and played with Mary Jane Lehmann, whom I would meet again, when we were eighteen, and I came back to N.Y.C. as a dead ringer for a limey, at least until I bought a pair of zip-fronted, tight pants and looked like a young man, not a Carthusian.

St Louis was where I spent my youngest years and I recall only the grass-banked streets, where stone steps went up to the porched houses with their deep inverted 'V' gables and their sash windows. My mother would take me to visit her friends after art classes. Once, I recall, a little boy came running from the back of the house, blonde and naked, and stood in the middle of the living room carpet and pissed on the Persian pattern. I can see him now, with his bold yellow arc in front of him, and the two young mothers gaping. I think I envied his impudence. He had a certainty about his claim to indulgence which I have never matched. I still think of him as the all-American kid. Even if we had stayed States-side, I should never have emulated his naked effrontery, but I might, I sometimes think, have been spared the education in shame which England confused (and often still confuses) with morality.

THE RT HON SIR DAVID STEEL PC, MP
Politician, journalist and broadcaster

Blocked by an Elephant

My father's church was based in Nairobi where he organized the creation of a splendid new building, now the very popular and crowded St Andrew's congregation of the Presbyterian Church of East Africa. He was also responsible, together with one colleague, in these early days for preaching intermittently at twenty-two different places throughout the three East African territories, and he managed to organize a lot of these 'safaris' during the school holidays, so that we all travelled with him. These were glorious and uncomfortable trips. The church, strapped for cash as always, had purchased what was euphemistically known as a safari car. In fact it was a Standard Vanguard van, with windows cut in the sides and a Dunlopillo mattress stuck in the back for the little Steels to sit on. Huge suitcases were piled high behind us. The East African roads were not in those days tarmac, and as the car bumped and slid its way across Africa the luggage careered forward pinning the wretched Steel children against the front bench seat. In these circumstances there was great competition to take turns at sitting in front between Mother and Father, the eldest son trying vainly to assert some rights of primogeniture.

These were memorable journeys. Both my father and his colleague were known to cover vast distances at reckless speeds, so much so that I recall the amusement in the congregation when, during a national road safety week, the sermon from the St Andrew's pulpit was on the text: 'It is Jehu, for he driveth furiously.' 'He's easy on tyres', one wag, it was reported, said, 'he hardly touches the ground.' On one occasion approaching the Tanganyikan coast near Dar-es-Salaam we came round a corner in a cloud of red dust only to find a lone elephant blocking the road and tearing at the foliage with its trunk. As we shuddered to a stop I was sitting in the back corner and I recall the terror as the animal turned and pawed the ground as though about to charge. Mother maintains that it had the largest pair of tusks of any elephant we ever saw, and we saw herds of elephants in East Africa. Wrenching one arm free from the mountain of suitcases which had of course descended on us I gently slid shut the side window for protection. I also asked for my camera which was in the glove box, but we were all told to be quiet. My father switched off the engine. The ear flapping and foot pawing act continued until disdainfully the elephant ambled off into the bush.

The Rt Hon Sir David Steel

COL JOHN BLASHFORD-SNELL MBE

Explorer

A Slobbering Dog

I can clearly remember the day when Father, a war-like Army padre, had returned from France in 1944 to disperse the rooks that were blocking the church gutters. This he had done with a rifle, to the detriment of the roof. My mother was also an exciting person. She adored animals and had kept a wild boar as a pet in New Zealand; twenty-eight cats, three dogs, a horse and a couple of foxes shared the Herefordshire vicarage where I grew up. One Christmas Day the Master of Fox Hounds called in for a port after church. He was a big, hearty man and had just emptied his second glass when he caught sight of the vixen asleep on the fireside mat. His monocle dropped from his eye.

'Oh my God, Vicar,' he groaned, 'the end is nigh, must be DTs at last.'

My parents looked up in surprise, but the MFH was already on his way out, muttering, 'Never thought it would come to this – bloody foxes everywhere.' He was gone before Mother could explain.

Brutus was a huge, stupid Saint Bernard, who roared rather than barked and would leap onto the garage roof to pull down my drying rabbit skins. He always won the fancy dress contest at the Church dog show and was a passable, if clumsy, gun dog. Unfortunately he couldn't tell the difference between rabbits, cats or small dogs and, one day, ate a poor, deaf old pekingese in the act of cocking its leg on the war memorial. I tried to comfort the grief-stricken owner by pointing out that the end had been both quick and painless and, anyway, the peke had had a good innings. Furthermore, I mentioned that my eleven-stone friend, who now sat beside me looking utterly dejected and dribbling with dismay, felt strongly about dogs of oriental origin desecrating a British war memorial. My reasoning was not appreciated.

Much of my childhood was spent in the company of this massive animal. He was at his worst in cars, slobbering abominably and frequently being sick, usually all over my grandmother and her cat. However, the good lady was of solid Jersey stock and, having been married to a John Blashford-Snell, had buried him and wed another, now deceased, before I knew her. Even a vomiting Saint Bernard did not deter Granny, who kept her false teeth in weak brandy at night and accompanied us on many wartime journeys in Britain, when we travelled in the wake of the 53rd Welsh Division in which Father was a chaplain. She also had a parrot. It was green and it swore, belched and bit. In short, it was a revolting bird which annoyed both my canine friend and my godmother, Aunt Jess.

Jessica Le Brun was quite a girl. Her medals told of proficiency as a nursing sister with the French Red Cross in World War I and her photograph album showed numerous handsome young men who had pursued her whilst she tore around Jersey in her AC sports car. Now, World War II had cut her off from her beloved island and she spent her time sticking pins into an image of Hitler and, in her spare moments, filling bombs with TNT in an armaments factory.

My mother's family was English and my grandfather, George Sadler, was a big, amusing man. Living the life of a country gentleman in a Suffolk village, he had engaged Zeppelins with his sporting rifle from the roof of the Hall in 1918, captured an escaped circus python with the tractor, almost killed the local vicar with a trick truncheon and collected a runaway bull on the bonnet of his Armstrong-Siddeley. His local hairdresser, on a rare visit to London, was amazed to be stared at by people whom he heard mutter, 'That's Barber Rowe from Braintree.' Convinced he was famous, the poor man was sadly shaken when he eventually discovered that George had pinned a notice on his back, which read, 'Barber Rowe from Braintree'.

Although I greatly admired George, I knew my godparents rather better. Lord and Lady Forester had travelled widely and it was their stories of big-game hunting and adventure that really made me long for a life of excitement.

My godfather was a soldier and had commanded the Royal Horse Guards. I often asked him where the German Maxim gun that was mounted at Willey Hall had come from, but he always smiled and just said, 'Something my regiment picked up in the Great War.' It was not until after he had died that I learned he had captured it single-handed. He had lived a wonderful life in the days of the Empire, hitch-hiking from Cape to Cairo, exploring the upper reaches of the Congo and, above all, devoting himself to the service of others. His particular love was Shropshire where he spent many years helping people and following his hobby as a naturalist and a sportsman. He lived out most of his final years in the other land he loved – Africa – and finally died peacefully in Rhodesia in 1977. The patience and understanding this kindly man showed me as a small scruffy schoolboy were to be a lasting inspiration.

I was also most fortunate to have a super aunt and uncle who lived in a cottage they had largely built themselves in the Welsh mountains. In those wild hills I could stalk rabbits with an air-rifle, watch tumbling miniature versions of the Victoria Falls and explore worked-out lead mines.

In the more sophisticated south, I had other relatives with vintage sports cars and a flair for practical engineering.

My *Just William* existence progressed through 'prep', a choir school in sleepy Worcestershire, where my voice had broken early, and where I learned poker in the commoners' stalls. At home for holidays, my musical enjoyment was confined to playing a drum, which made Brutus howl; a ghastly and unsociable noise. So I turned my attention to the church organ; alas, the organist was unsympathetic and, in a mood of sullen revenge, I took a rat that Granny's ginger cat had been gnawing in the wood shed and popped it down one of the organ pipes. With evil glee, I sat in the choir stalls next day, awaiting the awful noise that would result from the rodent rattling on the reed. However, it was not to be. True, there was a strange sound; then, oh horror, the rat flew out and landed on a choir girl's lap. 'Eekkk,' screamed the maiden and, unseen, I seized the creature and secreted it in my hassock. They all scolded the poor girl; no one believed her and I consoled myself with the thought that the rat had lived to be played another day.

My father, believing that I was a useless waster, encouraged me to do something positive to help at home. Therefore, with reluctance, I agreed to rise before dawn on Wednesdays and ring the church bell for mid-week early communion. The searing cold in the unheated rectory bit through me like an arctic wind, as I stumbled through the snow to open the heavy vestry door and tugged at the aged bell-rope. Even an illicit nip of Father's brandy did little to fortify me and I knew that if I were to survive, I must find a better solution.

It came to me like a vision – indeed it may have been divine providence that showed me the way. The great bell was within view of my window and I quickly discovered that a round of .300 rook rifle would produce a ring to waken the dead. Twenty shots and we had filled five pews, but alas, the resultant ricochets may have had more to do with it. As the last of the faithful scampered into the cover of the church porch, Father, in a biblical rage, reminded me that it was a house of peace. Nevertheless, he realized that we must move forward with the times and thus, by my next holidays, a gramophone and loud-speaker system had been installed to give a rendering of a slightly tinny version of 'Bow Bells' and other well-known peals. Not only did this increase Father's congregation, but when I turned the volume up to full power we even pulled in a few of the rival vicar's flock. Whilst fellow clerics muttered in the cathedral cloisters about progressive parsons, Pa enjoyed a full house.

In my new role as keeper of the records, I was responsible for this device. But, by now, I had grown older and had become friendly with the milkman's dark-eyed daughter, who sang in our choir. This temptress dared me to put a certain disc on the machine. Was ever Adam led astray by Eve? Thus, one day the parishioners were greeted with a jolly ballad, 'Captain Brown, Captain Brown, he played his ukulele as the ship went down'. In a final defiant gesture, I switched it on full volume to the deaf aid system for the last few bars, which sent the rows of pensioners bouncing from their seats.

It was perhaps understandable that my parents should encourage me to attend a school as far away from home as possible. Thus, in 1950, I arrived at Victoria College, Jersey. Granite-built, it stood fortress-like above St Helier. In the high windowed classrooms, generations of Channel Islanders, including my father, had studied hard to gain places in the establishments of the Empire and, also, for the chosen few, a venerated position in the dignified local government, the States.

In my spare time, I continued a scouting career in the school troop and rose rapidly to the rank of patrol leader. The Wolf Patrol, a strangely apt name for my group, were excellent air-gun shots, firelighters and trackers. However, a camp in Rozel woods with some enterprising Girl Guides did not altogether please our scout master, who gave us an afternoon's lecture on the facts of life and the sins of the flesh (although the milkman's daughter had beaten him to it!).

At this point I decided that if I were going to be licentious, I might as well do it properly, so I joined the school cadet corps. As cadets go, we were a pretty good unit. Our commander, Colonel Bill Eden, a firm but fair disciplinarian, had a flair for getting the best out of youngsters. He was also extremely keen on rifle shooting, which, being a major sport in Jersey, played an important part in our training. The island was full of retired officers who regularly shot alongside us in local matches. One eccentric major did much to encourage us and was also a source of amusement, especially when the aged spaniel, which always crouched beside him on the firing point, would break wind just as his master's watery, blood-shot eye had found the aiming mark and as he was in the very act of squeezing the trigger. The resultant shot would go wide of the target and, in a terrible rage, the major would boot the offensive animal off the point.

The occupation of the Channel Islands by the Germans in World War II was clearly evident: formidable concrete bunkers littered the cliffs, and the narrow valleys were a mass of tunnels. Guns, mines and all the paraphernalia of war were easily obtainable by adventurous schoolboys and how we survived was a miracle. Lugers were bought and sold in the changing rooms, Spandau machine-guns were stripped and cleaned in attics, whilst chemistry classes were essential for the understanding of bombs and explosives. At weekends we would cycle to remote areas to test our illegal toys. The absence of a paid police force in country districts greatly facilitated our pastime. Sadly there were accidents, some fatal, some almost fatal and others, simply hair-raising. As our knowledge of chemistry progressed, we learnt to make nitro-glycerine and, with this, blew open sealed bunkers in the search for more weapons and ammunition. Most of the nitro was made in a friend's greenhouse, because we believed that if it exploded we'd be better off inside, as presumably the glass would fly outwards!

In an effort to turn our minds to more peaceful topics, our headmaster, Colonel Ronnie Postill, created a compulsory debating society. Thus, all sixth-formers had to learn to speak in public, a valuable training that has stood many an old Victorian in good stead. To liven up our debates, a mock election was held. At once an evil bunch of us formed the 'Neo-Fascist' party. 'Nellie' Le Geyt became poet laureate and composed party political ballads, whilst Adrian Troy, Bungle Colson and John Gwyther became henchmen to myself as 'Blashford Von Schnell', the dictator. The population of Jersey was more than mildy surprised to see our Nazi uniforms, armbands and steel helmets. However, it was not until our storm-troopers raised a fourteen-foot German banner over the school that our patient headmaster intervened. Nevertheless, for weeks the election campaign raged with its incredible dramas and satire; mainly centred on the controversial problem of the emancipation of the mole. Mass meetings were held and hecklers dragged off screaming by my black-shirts to the showers, where they were treated to a cold wash-down fully clothed! Party songs were sung at midnight sessions in a secret beer cellar. It was all great fun and to everyone's horror, we almost won the final election.

KAYE WEBB MBE

Chairman and founder of the Puffin Club

And a Vicious Dog

he incidents that I remember most vividly from my early childhood are all gloomy; perhaps because it's more difficult to recapture scenes of happiness and contentment, and what shocks one as a child stays with one always. One occasion which I remember clearly was to do with a present. I was given a doll's pram for my third or fourth birthday and was promptly allowed to take my dolls out for a walk in it since it was a safe, quiet road. I started out happily and confidently, then half way along I stopped, frozen with terror. On the other side of the road a big black dog was looking at me – and I was very frightened of dogs. For what seemed a long time we stood and looked at each other, me with my pram, him presumably wanting a bit of friendship. And then he slowly and, so it seemed, menacingly (I can still see him doing it), crossed the road towards me, and I bolted. Abandoning the pram, I tore back to the house and stood shivering and miserable on the doorstep, watching him walk over and put his head right inside the pram and terrify my babies, but I didn't have the courage to rescue them. I have never forgotten that incident, or the legacy of guilt I have as a result of it.

A second incident also left me feeling guilty. I went to a nursery school in the morning where one day, seated around a big table, we were taught about the miracles of nature in terms of tadpoles which our teacher had collected in a big bowl. She was explaining to us how they would eventually become frogs. I became over-excited, leant on the table, the bowl full of water and tadpoles slid off it and broke, and the tadpoles were left waterless and squirming on the floor. Naturally I was scolded and told that I had killed these little living creatures and I never got over the feeling of being a small murderess.

Soon after I was four, I was sent to stay with my grandmother and three aunts in London because my mother was expecting a new baby. They were jolly, cheerful aunts, rather spinsterish except for the youngest, who was engaged to be married. During one jocular supper time they told me, as if it were a great treat, 'and you, Kaye, shall be Aunt Grace's bridesmaid.' 'What' I asked anxiously, 'does a bridesmaid have to do?' 'Oh, she follows Aunt Grace about, holding up her train,' they replied. I burst into floods of tears – it seemed to me that the very worst thing that could possibly happen, would be to spend the rest of my life carrying my aunt's train and not to live with my mother. It was like death. They couldn't understand why I cried. It wasn't until weeks later, when my mother saw me, and explained that it was a one day obligation that I recovered myself.

As a matter of fact, I never was my Aunt Grace's bridesmaid, because, even though I knew it was only for a day, I was prejudiced about the whole idea, so she married without me.

H. R. F. KEATING
Author

Bacon, a Sun Hat and Football Boots

here were good reasons for sending me away to boarding school at the age of six, but not being one of Nature's catchers-on I endured a curious existence for at least the first few terms I was at that prep school called Normandale.

There was, for instance, the business of bacon. We had bacon for breakfast, I suppose, twice a week. And at the table at which the smallest boys sat the headmaster's wife was accustomed to preside. Before her after the porridge had been dealt with was placed a large oval platter – I can see it now – filled with pieces of fried bread and bacon. The headmaster's wife, a notably kindly lady, would then put a piece of bread and a slice of bacon onto each of the pile of plates in front of her. As she did so, she glanced along the table to see which boy was to get the plate about to be passed down, and when she came to my plate she took care always and invariably to select the crispiest rasher in front of her.

Now the way I liked my bacon was not crispy. So it entered my confused six-year-old head each bacon morning that I had done something wrong. What that might be I had no idea – since I had little idea what in this strange world should be done and what not – but I knew, indelibly, that some wrong of some sort I must have committed, and that horrible, crispy bacon was my punishment for it.

I am sorry to say that some forty years passed before, with that morning scene suddenly flashing back to me, I realised that, of course, of course, the kindly lady at the head of the table had got it into her head that I liked nothing better than bacon crisply cooked, breaking into fragments at the touch of a fork. Nevertheless, out of purgatory – and purgatory it was forcing down those tough little fragments – comes at last a heaven. That lady, well-meaning, kind but atrociously muddle-headed, gave me many years afterwards a very decent suspect in my early detective novel, set in a prep school where croquet was much played, A *Rush on the Ultimate*.

The matter of the sun hat, however, I have never, even after more than fifty years, satisfactorily resolved. This was the situation: it was summer; cricket was, of course, played in the afternoon; generally, as the least aware boy on the field, I was placed at long-stop and happily dreamt away the long hours before the dreaded moment came of the side I was on having to bat and of finding myself eventually standing monstrously padded up in front of the wicket. But on this day, for some reason, I had been put to field at some other position, one where I was in some danger of having to make a catch should an ill-directed swipe come towards me. But, of course, I soon was away in some deep imaginary place – more or less the same place where I spend most of my time nowadays – and for some reason I chanced to take off the shapeless, grey felt sun hat with a narrow ribbon in the school colours round its non-existent brim, without which in the 1930s no tender middle-class boy was allowed to venture into the sunshine, and to hold it out, bowl-like, in front of me.

Well, yes, you have probably guessed what happened. Suddenly I was brought back to everyday reality by the thump of the cricket ball landing in my hat. But how did it get there? Was it truly that an ill-directed swipe had sent it curving through the summer air to just that spot? Or had the master in charge – I think it was Mr Peel – seen this boy palpably not filled with the proper team spirit and had decided to teach him a lesson by creeping up and dropping the ball into the extended titfer? I still don't know.

And was it a catch within the meaning of the M.C.C. rules or not?

But it was my first winter term that truly saw my downfall. At some time of the day, whether it was mid-morning or after lunch or at some other point I no longer know, if indeed I knew at the time, there would come a point at which every boy in the school was tumbled out onto the muddy playing field for a kick-about. Not a proper game, you understand, but just a general free-for-all to let off some steam. But this was, as I have said, the 1930s, when things were done the way they ought to be done. So even for those few minutes of exercise the proper boots had to be worn. There was a mad rush to the boot-hole – years later when I used this word in a short story for an American magazine, cables flew back and forth over the Atlantic seeking and offering explanation – followed by a wild scurrying as indoor shoes, objects distinct from outdoor shoes, were put into the appropriate cubbyhole and boots, proper football boots in rigid leather with solid leather studs in their soles, were taken out and rapidly put on.

Rapidly put on by every boy except Keating, youngest in the school. It was so difficult to ease the foot into the stiff leather – and then as often as not it turned out to be the wrong foot in the wrong boot – and then those laces, long and white originally, and needing to be pulled tight through all the lace-holes and finally wound twice round the top of the boot and tied with a neat bow, a bow which was meant to stay done up. No wonder the boot-hole was deserted by the time I had got through all that.

But get through it I did, and out onto the field I trotted, ready to do what I understood had to be done, or as much of it as I did understand.

And, sad, sad, sad to say, at once into the middle of my back there smacked a thick, heavy, mud-layered leather football booted with vigour by some huge twelve-year-old at the top of the school. End of sporting career. For ever, really.

H R F Keating

BOBBY ROBSON

Former England Association Football team manager and national coach

Take your Cap off to it

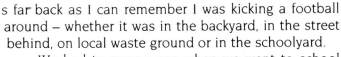s far back as I can remember I was kicking a football around – whether it was in the backyard, in the street behind, on local waste ground or in the schoolyard.

We had to wear a cap when we went to school and it would still be perched on my head when I was playing in football matches with other kids. But, when I was about to shoot for goal, I would quickly take the cap off. I think I became well-known for that idiosyncrasy!

As a professional footballer my biggest ambition was to play for England and win an international cap. I was fortunate enough to get my first one at the age of twenty-four. When I was England manager, I was responsible for handing out caps.

An international cap is not an easy thing to get and neither should it be. I stressed to each player in my England team that he had been selected because he was the best player in the country in that position at that time. Then he had to go out onto the pitch and prove it.

RACHAEL HEYHOE FLINT MBE
Journalist, broadcaster and sportswoman

Cricket Balls and Broken Windows

t was rumoured that I could score a cricket match competently before I could even string a sentence together in a school book.

I was only eleven when I went along to watch my father Geoffrey Heyhoe, playing cricket for the Technical College on a day when they were one man short. Amazingly, I soon found myself marked down to bat at number eleven for the college and had to go out to the crease to stave off defeat. The pads reached my waist and the bat felt like a tree trunk, but the men were kind enough to bowl me a few slowish half-volleys, and to everyone's surprise I managed to score two or three undefeated runs and save the game.

Back at school, I was chiefly restricted to the orthodox girls' games – hockey and netball in the winter, tennis and rounders in the summer. But things began to change when Lancashire-born Mary Greenhalgh, a representative cricket and hockey player, arrived to take charge of our PE department. In the summer of 1954, she took a somewhat rebellious school party to the Edgbaston Test ground to watch the Midland women's team play the touring New Zealanders. This was euphoria for me. Not only were we missing school lessons to watch cricket, but it was women's cricket, played at a very high standard.

As I studied the game that day at Edgbaston, I made up my mind that this was the life for me. Afterwards, we were allowed to go and meet the New Zealanders, and the autographs I avidly collected are still in my possession today. But I came away with more than signatures. I came away with an image of an exciting, challenging life, travelling the world playing cricket, meeting people. It seemed everything I wanted out of life, and I think it was there and then that I determined I must play cricket for England women – though, if the truth were known, I wasn't even sure whether England had a women's cricket team!

Looking back now at the team photograph of the 1954 Wolverhampton Girls' School cricket XI, it is interesting to find that I am one of three girls who in fact went on to play for England – an extraordinary achievement for a single school. The other two were Jackie Elledge and

Ann Jago (known to us all as Sago), great friends of mine long after we had all left schooldays behind.

If this was in fact the time when I decided my future, I certainly lacked nothing in the way of support and encouragement. My parents were, I believe, genuinely pleased at the sporting direction I had chosen, and my father would often spend hours bowling at me in the garden.

Our house seemed to be adopted as the sporting Mecca by the entire adolescent population of the road, but even when alone, I was never lost for something to do. I devised my own method of solitary practice, suspending a cricket ball on string from an overhanging plank attached to a low gutter, and patiently drove the ball backwards and forwards until my arms ached and the gutter nearly fell off.

Brother Nicholas and his friends at first tried to exclude me from their back-lawn cricket matches. For some time, I was delegated as preserver of the flower beds. In other words, they deigned to let me field, but refused me the chance to either bat or bowl.

After serving my apprenticeship in the covers, however, they relented and allowed me an innings, presumably with the conviction that it wouldn't last long anyway. I shocked them all by batting undefeated for three days and accumulating a score of about 380 not out. By the end of it, they were so frustrated – I think pride came into it, too – that they declared the opening of the football season and switched games, despite the fact that it was only mid-June.

Being four years older, Nicholas was able to bully little sister quite successfully. But he did, at least, teach me a great deal about courage.

I had to put up with such harrowing indignities as having the vacuum cleaner held over my head so that my plaits were sucked up to the machine. I had to join in crazy 'dares', which included jumping off a twelve-foot-high balcony on to a mattress on our lawn – only when our parents were out, of course.

Nicholas also involved me in his cycle speedway team, which he called the Penn Rockets, and he taught me how to ride a motor-bike. At least, he showed me how to operate clutch, gears and throttle and launched me off over the fields near our home. What he had omitted to explain was how to work the brakes!

Eventually, I became accepted by his mates, almost as one of the gang, although they insisted on nicknaming me Lizzie after that obnoxious Violet Elizabeth Bott in the Just William books who was always threatening to 'scweam and scweam until I'm sick'. To them, I had several uses, not the least important of which involved being sent round to neighbours' houses to retrieve lost cricket balls and footballs, exerting all my feminine charm!

The family on one side of us grew tired of our games and would often refuse to return the ball. But that was almost a relief compared with the house on the other side, where the people were friendly enough but their fearsome, vicious bulldog would threaten permanent damage to anyone who set foot on his territory. Duelling with that dog certainly sharpened up my reflexes – as it would have done for anyone whose job it was to bend down and find cricket balls under the rhododendrons with a snarling, snapping creature bearing down on one's seat at a rate of knots.

The garden games involved a simple system of scoring runs, including six if you cleared a fence or hit the house wall on the full or twelve if you cleared the roof. If you broke a window, however, you were out! Not only that, but you also abandoned your part in the game to race into town by bicycle and collect the necessary replacement pane of glass before my parents could discover any damage. I think our local glazier must have been familiar with every window pane in our house, and several surrounding houses, by the time we had grown up.

Rachael Heyhoe Flint

CHRIS BONINGTON CBE
Mountaineer, writer and photographer

Hampstead Jungle

 was brought up in Hampstead in a variety of flats around Hampstead Heath. The Heath was my wilderness and fantasy adventure ground from a very early age. I climbed its trees, terrifying my grandmother, ran away from home at the age of three with a little girlfriend, to be picked up by the police and rescued from the local police station later that day. As I grew older, it became a place to play upon, to wander in and to fantasise about. I drew maps of the Heath, building it into a gigantic wilderness. We had dens in Ken Wood amongst dense undergrowth in the forbidden part beyond the wooden palings that bound the paths. We discovered an exciting obstacle course between two branches of the woods which lie to the north of the Heath, and fought the occasional battle with youngsters from other schools – ones we all too often lost!

I still enjoy returning to Hampstead Heath but as with so many memories of childhood, I'm always amazed at how small it seems today and the fact that I can run round it in about forty-five minutes – and I don't run fast. And yet it still has the beauty, part inherent and part painted by the glow of nostalgia.

RICHARD ADAMS
Author

Bluebell Wood

 ne afternoon in April – I suppose I must have been about eight or nine – I was wandering down by the Bluebell Wood alone. On the east side there is open pasture land – a little valley with a rivulet – between this and the next similar but larger copse. I pottered along the eastern edge of the Bluebell Wood and there, on the bank by the south-east corner, I suddenly came upon what struck me then as an oldish man

Now when you met men on the Sandleford estate and you weren't on the footpath that crosses it from Wash Common to the Newbury-Southampton road (A34), they weren't as a rule friendly. You were trespassing. My father, being Dr Adams and well-known in the neighbourhood, could carry this off, but an eight-year-old on his own was another matter, as I had already had cause to learn. 'D'you know you're doin' wrong goin' across there?' I knew by sight the few men who worked in these fields and whom you were liable to encounter.

This man wasn't any of them and you could tell at once, by his look and bearing, that he wasn't. He would have been old for a farm labourer and besides, he didn't appear to be working on any sort of job. He, like me, appeared to be at leisure. He greeted me in a friendly way – I can't remember what he said – and although I didn't really know how to talk to him, except by corroboration and general amiability, he was clearly happy enough with my company and (unlike the farm labourers) wasn't particularly conscious of my being 'a young gentleman'. (Class distinctions were much more marked in those days.)

He was gathering twigs and lighting a fire under the bank – something I'd never seen anyone do before – and when we'd got it nicely going he proceeded to boil water in a somewhat old-looking tin can. When it boiled he made tea by throwing the tea in, chatting all the time in a kindly manner about nothing in particular, quite unlike any of the 'Jims' (workmen) I had ever met. We drank the tea black, though I seem to remember he had some sugar somewhere about him. When we finally parted – and I intuitively felt no suspicion or fear of him – I left him sitting contentedly on the bank.

He remains a mystery to me. Who – and what – on earth could he have been? He was not a tramp or any sort of vagrant; I am sure of that. Even at that age I knew what a tramp was like. They had a general air of resentment and unhappiness which made you sorry for them and angry on their behalf. They begged from you if they could. Besides, tramps stuck to the roads or to places, such as ricks or sheds, near the roads they had slunk off. They were unhappy. They told you about their bad luck. They called you 'sonny'. This man was happy enough, generous with his tea and enjoyed my company. He addressed me by no vocative at all. (I was sensitive to vocatives and unconsciously derived a lot from them about the speaker. 'Sonny'; 'young feller'; 'young man'; 'boy'; 'youngster'. Each of these implied something vague but valid. The one I always hated was 'old chap'. I still hate it and never use it myself. 'It's time you and I had a little talk, old chap.' 'Well, you know, old chap, that's not the sort of thing we expect.' My father would never use such a term: it was either 'Richard' or 'my boy' – which I was.)

Nor was this man a keeper. I knew about keepers, too. They were – and still are – authoritative in a deferential way (like warrant officers). They were usually dressed with a certain degree of neatness and propriety – I suppose, partly to reinforce the authority and partly as befitting the standing of their employer. As a rule they were crisp and sharp. They certainly didn't make stick fires and brew tea in cans. This man, whatever he was doing, was in no hurry and very much relaxed. He was wearing old, worn clothes, yet not the come-by garments of a tramp. Most striking of all was his manner, which was usually gentle. He didn't seem to regard our meeting as in any way odd. He made – he initiated – mild, trivial conversation. I never met him again – on the Sandleford land or anywhere else.

I have decided – or the best I can come up with after all these years is – that he was in some way connected with felling in the Sandleford copses. These – especially the Bluebell Wood – contained a lot of hazel, and it was the practice to cut this to the ground every few years – to harvest it, in fact – and then let it grow up again. This business, I rather think, was not carried out by the estate but 'sold' to people who specialized in it. I am inclined to guess that this unhurrying, kindly old fellow, taking his time on a pleasant afternoon, who had half an hour to brew tea and wasn't in the least bothered about who I was or whether I was trespassing , was engaged in some sort of examination or reconnaissance of the copses on behalf of the hazel cutters. They may have been based well beyond Newbury. That would explain this rather Edward Thomasesque encounter.

SIR CAMPBELL ADAMSON

Chairman, Abbey National

Fear of Fires

 still have an inherent fear of forest fires. It had been a very hot summer and I was taken by my parents to visit my sister, who was at boarding school in Surrey, and we went to have a picnic on the Hog's Back. As a well-brought up child, who had been told not to leave litter around, I took the small amount of litter across the road and set fire to it. Within minutes, because there was a wind, the fire was blown across the road.

I can see it happening now and I had started a forest fire of major proportions. For the whole of the rest of that day we tramped round the Hog's Back watching the firemen attempt to stop the fire which, fortunately, did not burn down anybody's house. However, repeatedly one heard other spectators of the fire saying that they could not understand how anyone could be so totally mad as to set fire to anything that day. I hung my head and walked away. I don't think I will ever start another one.

THE RT HON THE LORD DONALDSON OF LYMINGTON PC
Master of the Rolls

Scared of Snakes

any people are very frightened of snakes. I am one of them. But in my case I think that I know why. On a lovely sunny afternoon in 1926 I was sitting on a log watching my uncle digging the vegetable patch. I knew that he was an old man – at least forty – but very strong. I was fond of him and I thought that he was fond of me. Suddenly his expression changed to one of fury. The spade was raised above his head like an axe and he began to run at me. 'Run, run', he said as the spade came down missing me by inches. It missed me, but not the adder.

LESLIE THOMAS
Author

The Empty Day

 remember the first day I saw the Gaffer. It was in March and I had been thirteen a few days before. It was a day that held on to the tail of winter. An empty day with rain on the pavements and in the trees and in the sky. A small, pointed wind blew the rain into my face as I shuffled along from the station beside the man who had brought me.

The man did not talk. I kept up with him. I was carrying a blue sack, like a pillowcase, over my shoulder and it contained very nearly all I had in the world. The big houses in Gloucester Road stood vaguely behind their misty trees.

Towards the end of the road there shot up a sudden high wooden fence and I knew we had almost arrived. A few more shuffles and there was the gate. The man turned in and I followed.

Then I stopped. It may have only been for seconds, because the man was walking on. But I know I stopped and looked up at it. A quick loneliness came over me like a pain. No boy has ever felt so much by himself as I did in that moment.

I am not going to pretend that the years that followed were hard, or cruel, or even unhappy. This was not so. This could never be an Oliver Twist story or it would not be true.

But standing at the gate, in the drizzle, and the man walking ahead up the path unconscious that I had even stopped, left me afraid and wondering what was going to happen to me from then on.

The place filled the horizon. Yellow bricks and blank windows; a tower at the centre capped with a pointed roof, a horror built, it seemed, from some architect's nightmare. Across the front of the building were the words 'The Dalziel of Wooler Memorial Home' blazoned in golden letters, of all things, like an advertisement. In the middle of the tower, in more modest gold, was 'Dr Barnardo's Homes.'

I jerked myself to some sort of movement and followed the man who had brought me. He went up some stairs in the foot of the tower and I went in through the door after him.

We were in an entrance hall reeking of floor polish. There was a boy standing there picking his nose. The man told him to go and fetch Mr Gardner, the superintendent, and he went.

The man stood a couple of yards away looking around him. Drippings from our coats made liquid explosions on the red floor and settled like small rubies at our feet. The man still did not look at me, or speak. I might have been by myself.

Down the corridor echoed the Gaffer. He turned the corner of the hall into our view and approached with military stride and granite expression. He shook hands with my escort, a brisk once-up-and-down, and then led him into the office.

I remained there, still damp with rain and unhappiness, resting my blue bundle on the floor, and crooking a parcel of books in my other arm. With two fingers of this hand I hooked on to a small package holding a tin half-full of toffees. The full tin had been sent to me by an elder brother, just after my mother died, with instructions that half of the sweets were for me and the other half for my younger brother. I never heard any more from the elder brother, and I did not see the younger brother for another year and a half. Despite wretched and returning temptations I never ate the sweets. I kept them for him.

Standing in the hall was a little like being at the entrance to a temple, but with your nostrils full of floor polish instead of incense. Bootfalls and distorted calls sounded from the landing up inside the tower.

A few yards from where I stood there was a pedestal topped by a marble bust wearing a layer of dust and a slightly annoyed expression. There was quite a lot of dust clogging the inside of the eyes and I attempted to cheer my miserable self by trying to imagine what would happen if the head came to life and found all that muck in its eyes. I don't know who the head was – or if I did, I have forgotten – but the gentleman in the picture on the wall, the one with the watch-chain and the lion-tamer moustache, was Dr Barnardo, the Father of Nobody's Children.

TERRY JONES
Writer, film director and performer

The Alabaster Interloper

t is my earliest recollection. I am sitting in my pram with my brother. My mother, my dear mother, appears with some shopping, which she puts into the pram and then an alabaster bust of a girl.

I am shocked. Jealous. Offended. This strange, cold beautiful white head . . . is it supposed to be some replacement for my own dear warm pink mother? Why has my mother (of all people) placed this interloper in our midst? What can it all mean?

I begin to complain. But not only that, I take action. Without hesitation I rush to the defence of myself and my brother yes of even my mother herself. I am defending our family from this dreadful assault. I pick up the nearest weapon (a jar of marmalade) and hurl it at the hateful visage – so white, so beautiful, so cold and dead.

There is a satisfying crunch. I have chipped her nose . . . but my spirited defence is cut short by a horrified scream from my mother.

Suddenly I am a naughty, wicked boy. Doesn't she understand I was defending her? What was I thinking of? I was thinking of her, of me, of the horror of having a dead stranger (no matter how beautiful) and what's more, a dead cold stranger, thrust into our pram . . . into our cosy pram . . .

The memory fades. I only remember the poor alabaster statue sitting forever after on an obscure window sill with her chipped nose turned to the wall looking bashfully down in silent rebuke.

And my mother? Did she ever understand why I hurled the marmalade jar? I don't know. But I do know that I always remember those powerful feelings that I felt that day, whenever I am confronted by the apparently irrational tantrums of a two-year old.

THE RT HON PADDY ASHDOWN PC MP

Leader of the Social and Liberal Democrats

Tea with Edward Lear

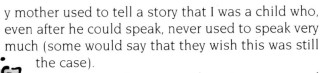y mother used to tell a story that I was a child who, even after he could speak, never used to speak very much (some would say that they wish this was still the case).

My parents apparently got very worried that there may have been a serious problem.

However, at the age of about five or six, we were visited by one of my uncles who had something of a reputation for eating a great deal. When he arrived we were all put on 'Family hold back' so that there would be enough for him.

On the particular occasion in question, he came to tea and I sat morosely at the side looking at a large pile of sandwiches vanishing rather quickly. Suddenly, this child who had said so little during his whole life came out with a complete stanza of an Edward Lear poem, which my father delighted in reading to us. I am told that I said, 'I thought I saw an elephant descending from a bus, I looked again and saw it was a hippopotamus, if he should come to tea I said (and at this point apparently I looked daggers at my uncle) THERE WON'T BE MUCH FOR US'. At which point I relapsed into silence amidst a startled family.

PROFESSOR HANS EYSENCK

Professor Emeritus of Psychology, University of London

The Future glimpsed in Sand

 only vaguely remember the following event which happened when I was about five years old, but several witnesses have repeatedly told me about the event in some detail. I was spending the summer holidays with my grandmother in Swinemünde, a well-known holiday resort on the Baltic coast. There was a competition to build sand castles, sponsored by the local Council, and to judge it they had invited Dr Eckhardt, very famous then as the Captain of the Graf Zeppelin.

My own effort was a rather poor one, but Eckhardt stayed to talk, and after a while had to be dragged away by his aides to carry on with his duties. Before leaving, however, he said to my grandmother: 'This boy will one day be a famous scientist!' What made him say this I cannot even imagine, but I have always remembered the occasion, and the words he said then. Prediction is always an uncertain business, and in this particular case I cannot think of anything I might have said or done that might have given him the slightest hint as to my future interests and possible successes. It remains in my mind as just one of those curious and odd things that happen, without explanation or meaning, but which nevertheless stay in the mind.

SIR YEHUDI MENUHIN OM, KBE

Violinist and conductor

A Sense of Vocation

was three years old and fortunate to be able to accompany my parents to afternoon concerts. On such an occasion I watched the concert master of an orchestra with intense interest, waiting for a solo passage on his violin as the sweet sound, thrilling, caressing and more entrancing than any other, held me captivated. After such a performance I asked my parents whether I might have a violin for my fourth birthday, so I could have lessons from this magnificent player who had so impressed me. I can only explain this request with having had a sense of vocation. Is this particular sense native to childhood itself? I wonder. Have the fortunate simply rescued from an otherwise lost age of innocence the conviction of unlimited possibility, the instinct for real worth, which make it easier for children to identify with great soloists or simple souls rather than with able middlemen?

I shall never forget my disappointment when a kind soul presented me with a toy violin. It is the only time in my life I can recall bad temper getting the better of me and I demolished this gift in the process. It was thanks to my grandmother that I, soon after, was the ecstatic owner of a real violin and to this day I am grateful to her – was it vision, generosity or recklessness? And the other part of my fervent wish came true too: I received lessons on this my first violin from that magnificent concert master, Louis Persinger.

SIR GORDON BORRIE QC
Director General of Fair Trading

An Early Concern

The fourth of my childhood holidays at Bexhill-on-Sea came to an abrupt end. On the beach on 3rd September 1939 I heard on the radio in our little wooden hut the ominous words of Neville Chamberlain that Britain was now in a state of war with Germany. Some time in the previous year – the time of Munich, I suppose – I had packed up as many of my precious toys as I could manage with a view to early departure from our home in Croydon. I must have understood then, at the age of seven, that my family felt war was likely to bring bombs to southern England and we should move to the north. That is what we did in September 1939 – 'we' being my mother, brother and two sisters and myself, my father having to remain behind and work in London.

My mother's favourite sister, Aunt Jane, lived in Colne in Lancashire and it was there that we went. Happily, Aunt Jane celebrated her 90th birthday four years ago and still lives in Colne. It was she who took me on a shopping expedition to Bradford that I remember to this day. It involved a gratifying long journey on the top of a bus, a slap-up lunch and cream tea and some serious shopping at Bradford's now extinct department store, Brown Muff's. I did not keep close to my Aunt. I ran up the down-escalator and down the up-escalator and was generally curious about the great range of items for sale. But I was frustrated. I was too short to see properly over the counters. Then I noticed that on each floor was a conveniently sited desk with pads of paper marked 'Complaints Forms'. I was soon busy writing out my complaint that the counters were too high, ending with my full name and address. Sadly, I never got a reply but I can date my concern for consumer rights from that day in Bradford in 1939.

SIR HUGH CASSON CH, KCVO, RA, RDI, RIBA, FSIA
Former President Royal Academy, architect, author and illustrator

Up the Creek

 ne summer my sister and I aged then about seven and eight went to stay at Sunbury on Thames with our Uncle Jim, as we did every year.

The house was large, a chauffeur was employed and, best of all, there was a boathouse containing a punt in which we were allowed to paddle about all day in the creek (though never in the main river).

In those days – the early twenties – campers used punts with green canvas hoods drawn over metal hoops for privacy and shelter leaving the inhabitants imprisoned like peas in a pod. At weekends clusters of these 'pods' were scattered along the creek and it was our innocent habit to scratch on the canvas and to question the occupants severely. 'Are you married?' was always our question to any couple and believe it or not, we were always politely answered and 'the ceremony of innocence', as W. B. Yeats put it, 'was never drowned'.

by Sir Hugh Casson

66

PRUE LEITH OBE
Cookery Editor, The Guardian

Here Comes the Soaking Bride

y brother David and I, when we were ten and eight, had a great game. We would hide behind the garden wall, and as cars drove down the road we would douse them with water from one of those old-fashioned fruit tree sprayers that you operated like a giant flit-gun. Most cars in the South African summer, before the days of air-conditioning, had all the windows open, and sometimes, which was marvellous, the target would be an open tourer or sports car.

By the time the occupants of the car recovered from the shock, and slowed down, gasping, they would be half-way down the road, the shower would be over, and they never came back to investigate.

One day, we had a bonanza. A wedding convoy led by the bride and groom in an open Rolls Royce, proceeded slowly down the road. We were merciless. First we soaked the bride, her groom, and the chauffeur, then set about the guests. None of the cars stopped, because, after all, they were in a procession and on their way to the reception.

But we had reckoned without the wit of the – presumably – best man and ushers, who were in the last car. They had ample time, with the ducking and weaving going on in front of them, to realise what was happening.

They stopped at our gate. Like terrified rabbits we just sat there, next to the bucket, incriminating spray in David's hands, waiting for judgement. And it came with a vengeance. One of the young men held me still while the other sprayed me from top to toe at point-blank range. Then they did the same to David, and finally up-ended him in the bucket of water. They didn't say a word. Just got back in their car and drove off after our victims.

BERYL COOK

Painter

The Favourite Game

y childhood is a long time ago, in Reading. Long walks with my grandfather, for which he supplied grey flannel trousers and walking sticks to my three sisters and myself. He also carried a big bar of chocolate which gave incentive to the flagging footsteps. Chocolate is connected with my mother too. She liked to eat this whilst lying in a hammock in the garden on summer Sunday afternoons, reading a magazine called *Red Letter* – remembered by me for their lurid covers. Her rest would either be accompanied by the sound of constant teasing and argument between us children, sometimes breaking out into violent fights, or moments of peace as we played a favourite game – climbing up and jumping off the top of a pair of step-ladders. Excitement would be added to this game if the boy next door decided to pick each of us off with stones hurled over the fence. He is now my husband.

JON PERTWEE

Actor

Time-Lord of the Flint Age

here was hardly any reason for our going further afield than the wonderful Caterham hillside to play. It was approached over a stile, and after continuing along the narrow path, it afforded a never-ending series of visual delights. The flowers were there then, the primroses, the violets and the most delicate of all wild flowers, the cowslip. Oh! Where have all the cowslips gone? I have seen nary a one in many years of searching.

As well as cowslips, snakes and swinging trees, there could be found flint, spear and arrowheads in abundance. There must have been a Flint Age encampment up there once and why not? It did not take much of a scout along its top-soil before, with a cry of excitement, another souvenir of centuries was kicked into the sunlight. Apart from the spear and arrowheads, there were the daggers, the cutting knives and the flint tools themselves that were used for the chipping and shaping. What a way for a small boy to be transported back through time! During these quests we transformed ourselves into grunting cavemen, and 'Woe betide any passing female' we threatened. She would've been grabbed by her long hair, dragged into our cave and hit over the head with a bone!

Further along was, to us, the most exciting place of all. Clambering over a locked gate and struggling through a dense forest of ancient yew trees, we came across our chalk-pit. It rose up from the edge of a 'jungle', like the temples in *King Solomon's Mines*. At its summit was a barbed-wire fence. A part of the First World War's defence against invasion, we were told. From the top, this fence protected our chalk-pit from further invasion, and there was no man, it seemed, prepared to risk his life, fighting through that impenetrable 'jungle' at the bottom. So the cliff lay before us to be explored. On our first visit we discovered, five feet up the cliff-face for all to see, a large and perfect fossil of an ammonite at least six inches across. From that day on with the aid of hammers and picks we collected dozens of near perfect specimens.

Along the hillside was the 'swinging tree', so-called for its near-horizontal branch of some twenty feet, with a small, dipped 'saddle' for sitting in at its end. Being only a few feet from the ground, the 'swinger'

– with hands on a lower branch – could control the ups and downs of the 'swingee'. The idea, as in all small boys' sports, was to flip the 'rider' off his 'Bronco', causing him as much grief as possible. My brother Michael and I became virtually unseatable, but the havoc we wrought amongst the local lads was legion.

In the 60s, when I came to live in the area again, my children and I rediscovered and 'rode' the 'swinging tree', but of the flints and fossils there was no sign. Had we taken them all, or had they shrunk back into hiding to await later discovery by a band of deserving lads who would really appreciate the finding?

Jon Pertwee

JEFFREY ARCHER
Politician and author

Unnecessary Obstacles

 think the most frightening memory of my childhood was a journey from Weston-super-Mare in Avon to Leeds in Yorkshire. The purpose of the journey was to visit an aunt and uncle who were school teachers in North Allerton and as I had never travelled beyond Bristol or Bridgwater I looked forward to the day with much anticipation and relish. My grandmother was one of those early drivers who did not require a licence and had she ever taken the test she would have undoubtedly frightened the examiner out of his wits.

We left Weston-super-Mare early in the morning in a large green Morris Oxford. My grandmother drove, my grandfather and mother in the back while I had the honour of sitting in the front, decades before anyone had thought of seatbelts. My grandmother like myself rarely travelled beyond the environs of Weston-super-Mare and for her the roundabout was a newfangled invention which she had not encountered before. We discovered the first one some seven miles outside my home town: she happily drove straight across the middle of it and carried on in a northerly direction. We encountered twenty-three such obstacles set unnecessarily in our progress, on our route between Weston-super-Mare and Leeds, and my grandmother crossed all of them in a manner which would have pleased Hannibal.

On arrival in Leeds my grandfather who had learnt several years before not to speak, my mother who was not listened to when she did and I, who did not murmur a word, breathed more than a sigh of relief when we eventually arrived at my uncle's front door in one piece. Once safely on the premises I ventured the innocent question of my grandmother, 'surely one should go around roundabouts and not across them' to which she replied with British certainty, 'certainly not. What you must understand young man, is that they will never catch on'; a degree of logic with which I am quite unable to find fault.

We returned home by train.

THE RT HON LORD JUSTICE BUTLER-SLOSS DBE PC
Lord Justice of Appeal

Lost Donkey

As a little girl I was given a soft toy, a donkey named Key, which went everywhere with me. My most vivid memory of my childhood was going at the age of three to Sheringham on the North Norfolk coast with my parents and my nanny. She and I went down to the beach to play, and Key went with me. I left Key behind on the rocks and did not discover my loss until we got back to the house. We could not return to look because it was by then high tide. I was inconsolable until Nanny said, 'Don't worry darling. Key will be there tomorrow morning. When it is low tide we will go down and get him.'

The next morning we went down to the beach and back to where we had played the day before. Wedged in among the rocks was a small, wet, much-loved toy donkey. I have him to this day.

MICHAEL ALDRIDGE

Actor

Aunt Edith's Lung

 think I first came to these parts, East Wittering, in the early thirties for a family summer holiday. We all loved it. It was such a welcome change from the 'bracing' holidays my father, who was a doctor, had insisted on previously. Norfolk or Suffolk – howling winds and freezing seas and little boys in Captain Webb-like bathing costumes with red noses and fingers white with cold and sea grass that stang and pricked the legs.

My much loved Aunt Edith – a kind and charitable lady – unmarried with pebble glasses and a tendency to deafness, who taught music, singing and pianoforte in Surbiton used, with mutual delight, to come with us. I remember, once, when shivering in the cold waves, Auntie, who was swimming some thirty yards away from us, singing out to us in her plummy contralto voice, 'Come over here everybody, it's lovely and warm!' My father looked across at her and said, 'Well it would be wouldn't it, she's swimming over the outlet of the sewer.' All that afternoon, whenever she approached us, my brother and I held our noses and said, 'Pooh'. She didn't mind, and I don't think she understood. She had a wonderful swimming action. It was the side stroke par excellence. One arm would be thrown vertically upwards like a periscope, and then as it descended she would sink below the water throwing a trail of bubbles to the surface, and then, after a surprisingly long time the arm would appear again followed by her face gasping for air. She was an avid helper in sand castle making and once, when leaning over to adjust a turret one breast inadvertently revealed itself. My younger brother about five years old, I remember, shouted with awe, 'Oh look everybody! Auntie's lung has fallen out.'

GEORGE MELLY
Jazz singer

Seaside Entertainment

here were other entertainments. The pier itself with its salt-corroded penny-in-the-slot machines. There was 'The Haunted House' and 'The Execution of Mary Queen of Scots'. Of these I preferred the latter: two doors slowly opening on the façade of a castle, the executioner bringing down his axe, the Queen's head tumbling into the basket, the doors banging shut. I was mystified as to how the head rejoined the trunk in time for the next penny. There was also a 'What the Butler Saw' machine. I enjoyed turning the handle very fast so that the fly-stained sepia image of a massive-thighed Edwardian lady was forced to remove her voluminous clothing at breakneck speed.

There was a concert party which, until I was old enough to understand the jokes, my parents enjoyed rather more than I did. What they liked was it being so hopeless. There was a sketch one year, an exchange between the 'light' and 'low' comedians about a family called 'The Biggers'. It described how the little Bigger had grown bigger than the bigger Bigger and so on. 'I see', said the 'low' comedian at the conclusion of this rigmarole, 'there's been a bit of bother at the Biggers'. My parents laughed so much at this that a young man, sitting alone in a deck chair in the row ahead of them, turned indignantly round and told them it wasn't kind to laugh at him just because he had red hair.

Sometimes I was put on a donkey but I didn't enjoy it much, especially when the donkey man would run with it jogging me up and down on its fat, yet bony, back. Nor did I appreciate being taught to feed a pony in a small enclosed field in front of our boarding house. My maternal grandmother, who was fond of animals, insisted I did this, balancing the lump of sugar on the palm of my hand, bending back my fingers to avoid them being nibbled. I can still feel the pony's wet, warm, snuffling breath and see its dilating hairy nostrils. Often I would drop the sugar but she'd make me start again. She believed, unlike my mother, in discipline or at any rate didn't lack the courage to apply it. My mother feared unpopularity, however short-lived, even from a child. 'When did you last punish George?' my grandmother asked her once. She couldn't remember.

They were happy holidays. I was the centre of attention, my every word repeated later to others in my hearing as though a miracle of wit or perception, every pose recorded by my mother's Brownie: the birds were fed on the biscuits they preferred, the stones were shifted, the water transported, and Punch was dragged squeaking and whacking his way along the road to perdition on the pebbly beach against the grey horizon.

As to why Llandudno comes back to me in such sharp focus from a time when Liverpool still seems fragmentary and vague I have, although it is apparently a common experience, no explanation. Perhaps the frame of the holiday, its yearly repetition clarified by growing terms of reference, developed and printed it in the dark room of memory.

George Melly

SIR RANULPH TWISLETON-WYKEHAM-FIENNES

Explorer, cameraman and writer

Disaster at Sea

hen Granny was alive we had never travelled far from Constantia. Now mother decided the family should see the Kruger National Park, so, with a couple of friends and all the girls, she headed northeast. At seven I was too young for the long journey and spent the holiday with a schoolfriend, James, by the sea. The memory of an incident at that time will remain etched on my brain as long as I live, as clear a vignette as that painted by Camus with his seaside murder in *L'Etranger*.

Making castles in the hot white sand at Betty's Bay, I watched a fat man rise sweating from his beach chair and trudge slowly into the breakers with a surfboard. He ducked and porpoised to less broken water further out, and I forgot him until his wife awoke and found him missing. I can see her homely face now as I pointed for her. Her husband was by then only a dark speck in the sea. A rescue boat was launched but they brought the man back dead, for he had let go of his board. Perhaps he had had a heart attack. When I smell seaweed or feel the heat of a long white beach I sometimes hear again the racking sobs of the woman as she knelt by the sandy body of her man.

THE RT HON KENNETH BAKER PC, MP

Chairman of the Conservative Party

Sliding down the Haystacks

 was at school in Southport during the war and still have a few memories of that time. We lived right alongside the beach in Southport. There was a golf course very close, but it was used to grow hay to help produce extra food for the war effort. When the hay was gathered in and made into haystacks my sister and I used to climb on them and use them as a slide which was tremendous fun!

Unfortunately, the more we used the hay as a slide, the more we wore the hay away, and this proved rather perilous because the farmer would try to catch us and chase us off. One evening my sister was stuck on top of a haystack when the farmer turned up. I had to try to distract him into chasing me away while she got down in safety. The simple strategy worked – but we had to help repair the haystack!

SIR MICHAEL HORDERN CBE
Actor

That little Roach

'm not good at dates, but I think it must have been in 1916. I'm not good at maths either but I reckon that would have made me five years old, though at seventy-eight now I remember the occasion as if it were yesterday.

We lived, a happy family, at Berkhamsted in Hertfordshire – 'The Poplars', High Street, Berkhamsted – and not far away, down between the High Street and the Castle ran, if that is the word, the Grand Union Canal. Horses plodding along the tow-path then of course (none of your smelly diesels), towing barges with their brightly painted living quarters for Mr and Mrs Bargee and family.

Now on this day my eldest brother, then and to this day known as 'Shrimp', a grown up young man of nine, took me fishing there for the first time. I can see it clearly still, I can see the clump of rushes on the water's edge beside me and my brother a few yards away on my right; I can see the painted float in front of me – placid and still on the surface of the canal – and then, mysteriously trembling, dipping, sliding, disappearing and with a shout from Shrimp my reflex action jerking from the water my first fish, my very first fish. A small roach I think it was. How I cried with the magic and thrill of it.

Of course, I wanted to take it home and show it to Mummy, but my big brother, who had actually fished on a trout stream, and had learnt to put small fish back, made me do so. More tears (my unkind elder brothers called me 'Streaks') but I was hooked, and of all the fish I have caught since – many is the roach, perch, carp, shark, sail-fish, trout, sea-trout and salmon – the remembrance of the catching of that little roach remains the most vivid memory. Oh! Happy Days.

I am going fishing with Shrimp this weekend. He's 82 now.

The Exploding dishwasher

ne of my happiest childhood memories was of the arrival of our first washing-up machine. This was an enormous stainless steel contraption which, I think, my mother had purchased from a catering company. It needed immensely careful loading and a highly trained operative to avoid disaster. Disaster was not, at the beginning, always avoided, nonetheless. The best occasion I recall was one where my father was giving rather a smart dinner party, as far as I remember aimed at impressing upon a visiting Australian agriculturalist that, though England might be small, it was not to be ignored in matters of agriculture. Things seemed to be going reasonably well until about the middle of the dinner when it became apparent that something had gone wrong in the next room where the washing-up machine was already in action. Unaccountable noises and splashings could not be ignored. Interrupting a dissertation on whatever it was – the farm price review and its inadequacies, I expect – my father opened the door to find a chest-high wall of soapsuds created by the dishwashing machine. Someone had filled it up with the sort of detergent that was supposed to go into the Bendix with wonderful results. I don't remember much about what happened next, except that it was all enjoyable.

THE RT HON JOHN WAKEHAM PC, MP, JP, FCA
Secretary of State for Energy

A Fascination for the Sea

 n the prologue to his famous novel *The Go-Between* L. P. Hartley wrote that 'the past is a foreign country: they do things differently there'. But my own experience has been rather the opposite. A strong sense of continuity still connects some of my favourite and most vivid childhood memories with the later pleasures of my adult life.

Above all, these memories revolve around sailing, and my continuing fascination for the sea.

I must have been about twelve when I first saw an advertisement for a Yachting World Cadet – then a new class of small sailing dinghy. It was the first, so far as I know, to be brought out in kit form, which was advertised as being suitable for construction by any reasonably skilled handyman (always provided that he had sufficient time available).

Since my father rather prided himself on his skills as a handyman, I unashamedly played on this by challenging him to build the dinghy. He readily accepted – too readily as it turned out. Living the very busy life he did, it soon became evident that he would not begin to have the time, and the task was eventually entrusted to the village carpenter.

I finally got my first boat, No 54 – which was coincidentally the same as our telephone number – at a cost of about £50. The carpenter proved more than equal to the task, and the dinghy which quickly took shape marked the beginning of my love affair with boats and sailing, which has continued to give me enormous pleasure for over forty years, and which still shows no sign of abating.

DAVID HICKS

Interior decorator, designer and author

Nobby

n the Easter holidays of 1944 I was very excited on going home from Charterhouse to get a surprise birthday present of a handsome new pony called Nobby, to replace Tuppence.

My mother was naturally delighted by my pleasure and a few days later I rode over to a Pony Club gymkhana at Earls Colne some six miles from Little Coggeshall. But such a long hack was well worth while on my lovely new pony.

Imagine my trauma when Rachel Gosling yelled at me, 'What are you doing on Greyling?'

'It's Nobby,' I said proudly.

'Rubbish child. I'd know Greyling anywhere – let me look at his teeth. Your mother's been sold a stolen animal!'

I think she reduced me to tears.

A few days later cheques were returned and made out differently, but he remained Nobby for the rest of his time with us.

KEITH WATERHOUSE FRSL
Author

A Precocious Career

I arrived at my council elementary school on a Leeds housing estate a precocious four-year-old and left it a precocious fourteen-year-old.

In the intervening years I was intolerable. I went through my schooldays convinced that I was the cleverest boy in the school – which, if cunning is another word for cleverness, I was.

I was astounded and hurt if I did not come top in examinations, for I was a brilliant and audacious cheat. For conventional studies I had no time at all. My only aim was to demonstrate my superiority over all those who were ill-starred enough to be my teachers, whom I arrogantly regarded as morons. It is astonishing that I survived.

I was allowed to join the infants' class two terms early by reason of having harassed my mother to distraction by prematurely reading books. A self-taught four-year-old among a class of five-year-old illiterates is off to a head start. No wonder I was insufferable.

I won my first school prize at the age of six. Our teacher, a Miss Pease, turned up on the first day of term with a ceramic salt, pepper and mustard set in the form of a donkey and fruit-cart. I don't know how she came by it or what possessed her to offer a cruet as a suitable prize for children barely weaned off rusks. But offer it she did. It was to go to the boy or girl judged by Miss Pease to have been the best-behaved during the term. I determined to have it.

So did all the other children in the class (so maybe it was not such a bizarre choice after all). But I was smarter than they were. I reasoned that being of such tender years they would quickly forget why they were behaving so nauseatingly well, and would lapse into their old ways. I, however, would remember. Instead of wasting my energies being indistinguishably well-behaved along with everyone else, I would continue routinely creating havoc until the last couple of weeks of term, by which time all my classmates would have fallen by the wayside. I would then bring myself to Miss Pease's attention with a quick spurt of angelic behaviour, and so win the prize. The ploy worked. I bore the donkey-and-cart cruet home with smug pride and it stood on my mother's mantelpiece for twenty-five years.

Moving up to the junior school was an unsettling experience, for the junior school had male teachers, many of them said to be of a violent disposition, and I was not sure that they were to be bamboozled as easily as the ladies in lilac smocks I had led by the nose in my spectacular career in kindergarten.

I decided to put the issue to the test at the earliest opportunity. Positioning myself outside the junior school staff-room, I chalked on the wall in six-inch-high letters the legend KW IS A FOOL. And then waited for a teacher to emerge. As it happened, it was the headmaster himself who came out first. Quailing inwardly, I regarded him unblinkingly as he stared distastefully at my graffiti.

'Is that your handiwork, boy?'

'No, sir.'

'Don't lie to me, laddie! You still have the chalk in your hand!'

'But sir!' I piped up, all injured innocence, pointing to the KW in KW IS A FOOL. 'Those are my own initials. I'm not likely to call myself a fool, am I?' Thwarted by this piece of warped logic, the headmaster strode off without another word. Brandishing my chalk, I turned back to my handiwork and thickly underlined it for good measure, assessing correctly that he wouldn't remember whether it had been underlined or not.

In junior school I learned how to win at exams. The more spectacular the crib, I found, the less likely it was to be detected. Teachers were always on the look-out for history dates scribbled on thumb-nails or on bits of stamp-hinging wrapped around inkwells. They were not on the look-out for history dates meticulously copied out to resemble a school timetable and then pinned to the class notice-board – which happened to be next to my desk. I put no little effort into cheating at exams – far more than I ever did into swotting up for them – and I regret to say that I have never felt the slightest twinge of guilt at thus beating classmates academically abler than myself.

My most famous coup was to cause an end-of-term geography paper to be 'lost', so that I had to sit the examination again. By that time, of course, I had mugged up the answers. But to allay suspicion I was careful not to get every one right, so that I came not top, but third. Such subtle manoeuvres, while doing little for the soul, must at least have been useful for exercising the intellect. More fruitful, I believe, than learning the principal rivers of Australia.

I think I will draw a veil over my three years in senior school. I was bolshy, cocky, overwhelmingly conceited and a considerable pain in the neck, especially to my English teacher, with whom I used to argue insolently about syntax. Probably to his relief, I discovered the delights of playing hookey. A playground fall had resulted in my having to report to the City Infirmary for a series of X-rays, and I had had the foresight to retain the last of my official appointment cards demanding my presence on Friday at 3pm. But it didn't say which Friday. Over a period of two years, brandishing my grubby exeat, I would periodically skip Friday afternoon English classes and take myself off to the pictures.

Years later, when as a reporter on the local paper I went back to my school to cover some function or other, I confessed to my English teacher.

'Yes, I know,' he said. 'You were seen more than once going into the cinema.'

'Then why didn't you do anything about it?'

'We didn't want to cramp your style,' he said. And it wasn't until then that I realised my teachers knew more than I thought about teaching.

Chris Bonington

Terry Jones
(right)

Col John Blashford-Snell

Ruth Rendell

PROFESSOR J. M. WARD, AO, FASSA, FAHA, FRAHS

Former President of the Royal Society of Chemistry

The School Explosion

hildhood is a time of wonder, and the wonder revealed by a toy microscope, a chemistry set or a colourful classroom demonstration has fired many with enthusiasm for science.

For me that fire came in the final stages of childhood. I was fifteen, one of four who constituted the Lower Science Sixth. One of us was given the title of laboratory steward and paid seven and sixpence a term for preparing the teaching demonstrations and for keeping the reagent bottles charged and clean. As he was the smallest, we had the unlawful run of the chemistry laboratory after school to make our own fiery and explosive experiments. One of the best was to make nitrogen tri-iodide. When you first made it you had a wet, muddy brown mess, but after you left it to dry overnight, it exploded at the gentlest touch with a heartening crash and an ascending purple cloud of iodine vapour.

One morning I was puzzled to find in the corner of a small adjoining preparation lab. nothing but a faint brown stain on the floor where I had left a larger than usual charge to dry. I resolved to thump the laboratory steward for taking fright and clearing it away after I had left but I soon forgot it. During mid-morning Maths the Lower Science Sixth were summoned one by one to the laboratory where the senior chemistry master sat at his desk on the dais as if understudying for the Last Judgement. Before him the second form sat at the benches, their unheeded text books open in front of them. Beside him, anxious and pale, the laboratory steward and his assistant (two and sixpence a term).

'Ward! did you last evening manufacture any nitrogen tri-iodide?'
'Why Sir?'
'Because Ward, the charlady swept it up and is now stone-deaf.'
'Oh Lord, Sir!'
The dire news was allowed to take its full effect, then,
'Ward! have you manufactured nitrogen tri-iodide previously?'
'No Sir.'
A lie and a fatal error for I was told repeatedly afterwards by the science master and then by the headmaster before I was beaten with many stripes, that had the poor lady tried to pick up my preparation

she would have lost her fingers. It was then too late to reply that if that were so my right arm would by now finish at the elbow.

For a worried few hours I wondered what total deafness was worth in damages, then I was told that predictably and fortunately the charlady's deafness had passed. Less predictable was the adulation by the Lower School. Fired by imaginative reports from second form witnesses, excited juniors ran up with, 'Ward, did you really blow the charlady's leg off?' or, 'Ward, is it true she gave birth on the spot?' Like many a young pop musician, the adulation proved to be too much for me and I felt that if chemistry could produce such glory I must have more of it. But of the many spectacular experiments I have made, at the Chemical Defence Experimental Station, Porton, during the war, and afterwards among the fierce furnaces and high voltages of the Electricity Supply Industry, none has brought such instant recognition.

ALLAN GREEN QC

Director of Public Prosecutions

Elusive Justice

n most people's recollections of their childhood, school days inevitably loom large. Looking back on mine from the comparative haven of middle age, I can say with certainty that they were not the happiest days of my life; nor were they particularly wretched.

A few bizarre characters and incidents stand out. I went to my final prep school, Hazelwood, as a boarder in 1945. There I met the master whom I recall vividly as the finest teacher I have ever encountered. He was an eccentric, bibulous Irishman named Wright whose teaching of Latin and English was inspired; he composed verses and parodies in both languages that I still remember today. The headmaster was called Ellis Parry. He read aloud superbly and on Sunday evenings the older boys would gather in his study – the most senior on chairs, the rest on the floor – and he would read some Conan Doyle or Buchan.

On one occasion a boy stuffed a rag down the lavatory and blocked it. Parry threatened to beat the whole school if the culprit did not own up. He waited in vain for a confession and then proceeded to carry out his threat. When my turn came, he candidly acknowledged that I couldn't have been responsible since I had a perfect alibi: I'd been in hospital, having ruptured myself lifting the school tea urn. Nevertheless, he had said he would beat everyone and he did. This convinced me that justice is elusive.

When I was about thirteen I first went to court, accompanying a litigious grandfather. He sued or was sued many times in his life, and he invariably lost. His counsel on this occasion was Leonard Caplan, then a 'rising junior', whose urbane tenacity impressed me enormously and put the notion of a career at the Bar into my head. To a garrulous and gluttonous schoolboy, being paid to talk was almost as attractive as being paid to eat or drink.

At Charterhouse I acquired an enduring love of music, but I was a hopeless performer. Having heard my efforts on the flute, my teacher suggested that I should transfer my attention to the euphonium. This turned out to be a mistake. I played no better, and the instrument was much heavier to carry and far more trouble to polish. My attempts to dance were equally unsuccessful. My father alleges that I took six lessons in one day (at Eve Tynegate-Smith's school in Baker Street where I was taught by a pretty girl with lots of green eye-shadow) and that he found me at home waltzing with a chair. I still can't dance a step.

THE RT HON THE LORD GRADE OF ELSTREE

Chairman, The Grade Company

Feeling the World open up

was five and a half years old when I came to this country from Russia with my parents and my younger brother Bernard (now Lord Delfont).

I couldn't speak any English at that time but, living in an environment with people of similar backgrounds, communicated in our common tongue of Yiddish.

Gradually I learned English, but until I had mastered it fairly well, I was unable to go to school. By this time I was about eight years old, and when I went to school, I was put into the Infants' Class. But after six months I was moved into a higher grade, where I mixed with boys of my own age and older.

This was such an exhilarating and exciting time for me. I loved school and made many friends, and indeed kept up a relationship with quite a number of them for years after leaving school. I found I had an aptitude for short distance running and I enjoyed learning different things – feeling the world opening up for me.

I was particularly fortunate in having a headmaster who took a special interest in me. He discovered that I had a talent for Arithmetic and encouraged me to develop it, which seemed to indicate that I would finish up being an accountant.

However, Fate decided otherwise. I am now eighty-two and still heavily involved in the entertainment industry, and I intend to continue working for as long as I am able. But I still look back on my schooldays with great nostalgic pleasure, and whenever I am asked to detail my background, I always give the name of my educational training as Rochelle Street School – my very first and only school.

THE RT HON LORD JUSTICE WOOLF PC

Lord Justice of Appeal

A Youthful Indiscretion

aving been appointed to conduct an Inquiry into disturbances in prisons, a reporter was provoked to investigate my past. There duly appeared a report in the paper that I had once spent a night in police cells. I was, of course, wholly innocent. It happened in Trafalgar Square on Guy Fawkes Night. The police were, not unreasonably, feeling somewhat frustrated by a horde of students who had blocked Trafalgar Square in order to protest at the cancellation of their Guy Fawkes celebration. An over-energetic policeman almost knocked my girlfriend over, and at the age of eighteen, being more gallant than discreet, I tried to insist that he should apologize. The result was that the officer said: 'We will have him', and three of them did so, but not before I had succeeded in making one or two points which resulted in my photograph having a conspicuous place in the morning papers.

I spent the night at the up-market Saville Row police station and next morning appeared before Bow Street Magistrates. After the wrong charge of indecent behaviour had been amended to alleged insulting behaviour, to the dismay of my friends who were looking forward to my displaying my limited capacities as an advocate, I pleaded guilty. I was fined a relatively nominal sum.

I thought little more of the incident until twelve months later. I was due to travel round the States and needed a visa for this purpose. My application required me to disclose my offence. This resulted in my being summoned before the Vice-Consul who was extremely attractive and who had recently arrived from the States. She wanted to know whether my offence was of a political nature. I had to confess that it had political connotations because, at the time, I was demonstrating at being prevented from celebrating an attempt to blow up the House of Commons. The Vice-Consul had not heard of Guy Fawkes! The result was that I was able to give her a protracted lesson in English history over a number of drinks at a celebrated pub in Shepherd Market. This led to a rewarding long friendship. The moral of the story – crime sometimes pays!

SIR RICHARD GASKELL

Former President The Law Society of England and Wales

The Evacuation

t the beginning of the last war, my father, a doctor, volunteered for army service as his doctor father had done a generation before. He moved my mother, my two sisters and me with our nanny to his parents' house in Budleigh Salterton in Devon where more over-ninety-year-olds were reputed to live than anywhere else in Britain. It was a large house with plenty of room for us all.

The war had little effect on the town but the occasional air raid warning would send us scuttling to the billiard room in the basement, there to spend time until the 'all-clear' sounded, huddled in our sleeping bags under the billiard table.

A boy from the East-End of London suddenly joined us as an evacuee. It must have seemed a rather curious household. We children spent our time, when not at the local dame school, in the day nursery or in the large garden, but we were taken to the drawing-room (heated by about three pieces of coal) for the evening ritual of the six o'clock news with my grandfather, who spent most of his time firmly shut in his study. After the news he would open the drawing-room windows leaving the family in 'healthy fresh air' while he retired once more to the unhealthy warmth of his study. The evacuee lost no time in finding the economic possibilities; he searched my grandfather's dressing-room, found his gold half-hunter pocket watch, purloined it, was found out, and was on his way never to be heard of by us again.

It was a house in which we were brought up not to use bad language, nor was it ever heard. As I walked to school I saw each day two first floor windows, one of which bore the legend in gold letters 'Solicitors' and the other 'Commissioners for Oaths'. I didn't know, and at that time I didn't care, what Solicitors were but with the wisdom of a child I knew that the others were special people to whom you could go to use bad language and feel better!

I was not to know that I should grow up to become a Solicitor and a Commissioner for Oaths. Had I guessed it I would not have thought that I would become President of The Law Society.

THE RT HON DAVID OWEN PC MP

Politician

Raison d'être a Ration

 ne day in the autumn of 1945 I was summoned by the headmaster, who told me to go to the front porch as my mother and sister had come to take me out. With them was a strange man with a moustache. I went up to them, shook hands with the stranger who asked me my name. 'Owen, sir,' I said. 'In that case I'm your father,' he said. He had just been demobilized from the war. Our relationship then got off to a bad start. We went to lunch at a local pub. This was a time when rations were still very short. To my delight, I saw that spotted dick pudding was on the menu. Raisins were a luxury. When it arrived, I picked out all the raisins and carefully put them on the side of my plate to have as a marvellous treat at the end of my meal. I had just finished the pudding, and was gazing at my raisins like the fat boy in *Pickwick Papers*, when suddenly my father leaned forward, put out what seemed to me an enormous hand, scooped them up and ate them. It was years before I believed that my father, seeing me extract the raisins and put them on the edge of my plate, concluded I didn't like raisins, and that since he did, *he* would have them.

THE RT HON SIR PATRICK MAYHEW PC, QC, MP
Attorney General

A Brother's Tragedy

 n November 1943 I was fourteen, and in my first term at my public school, Tonbridge. One morning, I was sent for by the headmaster, who was also my housemaster. I duly entered his study. The sun streamed in through the great windows, beside which tall yellow and white chrysanthemums stood in their pots.

'I have very sad news for you, Mayhew', he said, 'your brother has died of wounds in Italy'.

'Oh! I see, Sir', I replied, and wondered how the interview would end. I decided to stare at a vase on top of a tall bookcase until something happened.

For at least half a minute nothing did, and I stared resolutely on. Stick it out, I thought, and you will get away without embarrassment. Then the headmaster, a grave but kindly man with a Military Cross won in Flanders, said he believed I had known that my brother had been wounded.

'Yes, Sir', I said, for I had known for five stomach-churning days.

'Well, you will be collected at 12.30 pm by . . .' – he named a family friend – 'to go home for three days'.

I released the vase and fled.

As I made my way along the stone passage to the boys' side, I paused at a point which I can identify precisely today. I would, I there vowed, avenge my brother's death by killing – yes, *six* Germans. I recognised, at the time, that the calculation was rationally unsustainable, yet somehow it seemed right.

Grief followed very soon, intense and innermost. One night, in the dark, I knew with certainty of my brother's presence beside my dormitory bed.

Services in Chapel – 'succour the wounded, comfort the dying' – were bearable only by dint of silent and sustained cursing, head down and teeth clenched.

To my heartfelt relief, neither the Chaplain nor anyone else tried to be pastoral. Today, this seems extraordinary. The sole reference to my only brother's death was made by a contemporary in the Studies.

'Bad luck, man', he said. Embarrassment made any acknowledgement impossible.

The young, nowadays, behave naturally and do not require themselves to do otherwise, and I am glad of it. It was very different nearly fifty years ago.

As for my vow, Nazi Germany was defeated within eighteen months, before I could enlist. I rather hope, however, I had discarded it by then.

ALAN BOND AO
Chairman Bond Corporation Holdings

Recovering Father

f course I have memories of a childhood which seemed almost totally occupied with London during the Blitz of World War II. It was an unforgettable time for children but very difficult, I am sure, for our mothers who had to struggle on without fathers who were away at the war.

Indeed, my most vivid recollection of my birthplace was standing on the platform at Waterloo Station waiting for the train to come in with my father who was being repatriated home from the front.

When I had last seen him a couple of years earlier he was still a great athlete and very much sports oriented. He was a physical training instructor before and during the war and spent some time training commandos.

So that when he went away he was fine and strong and I was immensely proud as he waved goodbye to my mother and my sister.

He stepped slowly from the train into our arms a man near breaking point. He had travelled rough and fought hard, at one stage with the Australian soldiers besieged at Tobruk. When he finally decided to leave England for a better climate in Australia he was a TPI (Totally and Permanently Incapacitated). But the family all felt he had a chance of at least another couple of years of life away from the fogs and smogs of London.

Once he had established himself in Australia he arranged for us to travel as migrants to join him. And when I walked down the gangplank at Fremantle (Western Australia) it was a much happier father greeting me. He had taken up swimming and we set about rebuilding our lives on what we had originally believed was my father's borrowed time.

When people ask me what it is I love about Australia I tell them that it gave me another twenty years of life with my father. It's something that is beyond price to any son.

PAUL NEWALL, TD, DL

Alderman, City of London and Sheriff

The Clarion Call

Most vivid is my memory of Winston Churchill visiting the boys at Harrow, on his birthday.

To an impressionable sixteen-year-old, the sight of that greatest of Englishmen joining in the songs of his old school in the great hall of Speech Room, with tears rolling down his face, was unforgettable. After songs he spoke to us, to six hundred young men in that troubled year of 1950.

His message was simple but electrifying. I will try and quote:

'*You* are the vanguard of the youth of this country. In these uncertain times *you* are the hope for the future. Go out and lead! – and may God bless you all.'

It was a clarion call, and no one in that room could doubt it.

Afterwards, we crowded into the night, into the narrow street outside, and when he appeared on the balcony of the headmaster's house, the cheer that went up was wild, and six hundred straw hats soared into the night sky.

Prue Leith
(far right)

Michael Aldridge

Sir Michael Hordern
(centre)

THE RT REV DR GEORGE CAREY

Bishop of Bath and Wells, Archbishop of Canterbury Designate

Future Archbishop Pinches Bible!

y family was bombed out during the war and we went to live in Dagenham in Essex. I grew up on a very large Council estate and I recall very vividly an incident that happened when I was about eight years of age.

One afternoon I was playing with my friend Alec when another friend rushed along and shouted excitedly:

'Hey, guess what! There's a freight train over by the Ship and Shovel and, you'll never guess, it's full of Mars bars!'

'Mars bars,' Alec and I exclaimed in unison, 'That's great!'

'Let's go and have a look,' said Alec, 'You never know we might be given a bar or two!'

So in the early evening three small boys went to the waste ground by the pub the Ship and Shovel where, sure enough, a train was standing idle. We crept along the side and we noticed a door was open.

'Coo' said our friend, 'Look! There *are* Mars bars!' And peeping inside we saw in the carriage a number of great boxes.

By this time our imaginations were working overtime and so three sweet-starved youngsters clambered aboard drooling at the prospect of unlimited Mars bars to eat.

'Let's open a box!' Did I hear my voice cry that?

No matter. Soon a box was torn open and then two things happened almost simultaneously. First, Alec cried in disgust: 'These aren't Mars bars – they're books!' The other thing, much more terrifying, was that a shadow appeared from the corner and a man's deep voice boomed: 'What are you kids doing here!'

We turned to run but I was too late. A hand fell on my shoulder and I was dragged into the sweaty embrace of the elderly night-watchman. I squealed in fright, 'We were only looking for Mars bars, Mister!'

'Mars bars? You young blighters! There are no Mars bars here.' And reaching for the box that Alec had opened he revealed a number of books that were clearly marked for a library somewhere. 'Here', said the man reaching for one of the books, 'Here is one that will do you a lot of good,' and he waved a bible under my nose and sent me on my way with a clip round the ear.

Looking back forty-four years I am sure it has!

GERALD SCARFE
Artist

Collecting Acorns

 was born in St John's Wood, London in 1936. My mother was from Radnorshire and had been a schoolteacher before her marriage. My father, a Londoner, spent all his civilian life in banking. From the age of one I suffered from chronic asthma. I was three when the war broke out and my father joined the Royal Air Force.

We were living in Goldhurst Terrace when the air raids started on London and when the siren went and the bombs began to fall we sat in the cellar. I was frightened of the claustrophobic Mickey Mouse gas mask I sometimes had to wear.

My father was posted to Shaftesbury within a year and my mother and I followed to the comparative safety and bliss of the Dorset countryside. I have memories of walking with my mother down golden brown country lanes in the Autumn sunshine collecting acorns for pigs as part of the war effort and eating dried eggs and dried bananas. My mother saved me all the family butter ration to 'build me up'. I hated it. I preferred margarine.

NED SHERRIN

Film, theatre and television producer, presenter, director and writer

Cue Cowslips

A green field covered in cowslips. A small boy just over two years old. An indulgent aunt. Together they pick the flowers until the boy is bored. The aunt demurs. The boy surveys the carpet of cowslips and says with awful cuteness, 'We must leave some for another little boy to pick for his mother'.

I have been told this story so many times that I now believe that it is my earliest memory. However, it is no longer possible to distinguish between the event and the account ... but my infant instinct to find an excuse for going home which would leave me in a better light rings true.

The green field lay between the villages of High Ham and Low Ham, on part of my father's farm, Gawler's Farm, in Somerset. We left it in 1934 when I was three.

Two authentic memories. The first visit to the new farmhouse still occupied by the previous tenant – tears and disgrace. Then, moving into the new home which was much larger, an old coaching inn at Kingweston. I ran lost around the unfamiliar stone passages crying, 'Mummy, where is I? I's lost.' The dialogue is perhaps too fey to be true and the grammar may have deteriorated in the years of indulgent retelling; but that is how I recall it.

MICHAEL HOLROYD CBE

Author

Something Lacking

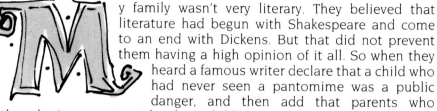 y family wasn't very literary. They believed that literature had begun with Shakespeare and come to an end with Dickens. But that did not prevent them having a high opinion of it all. So when they heard a famous writer declare that a child who had never seen a pantomime was a public danger, and then add that parents who thought it wrong to take their children to the theatre were highly responsible, they resolved to do the right thing. In short, they asked *my aunt* (who had a subscription at Boots the Chemist's library) to take me to a local pantomime.

I had been on a few literary expeditions with my aunt before — most notably inflicting books on German prisoners-of-war. Since I was an only child and brought up in these years of the Second World War largely by grandparents, the thought of this adventure filled me with intense excitement. I felt dizzy. We set off by bus, arrived in good time for the matinée, ordered our trays of tea and biscuits and ice cream, and settled down for our entertainment. I had no clear idea of what this entertainment might be — except for one thing which I knew for certain and waited for impatiently. But the show baffled me. I couldn't get hold of the plot, or understand why it was so often interrupted by incomprehensible jokes and silly asides. Even the actors and actresses (it was not easy sometimes to tell them apart) didn't seem to believe what they were doing. Perhaps they found it as difficult to follow as I did.

In the interval I cross-questioned my aunt, but she appeared vague, almost as if she didn't know what I was saying. I sat through the second half with rising dismay and suspicion, and at the end I felt bitterly disappointed. What had gone wrong? Were they ill? There had been no pandas at all — and what was a 'pandamime' without pandas?

SIR DAVID NAPLEY

Former President The Law Society of England and Wales

The Finest Performance

y father was an exceptionally able pianist, a skill which, to my great regret, I did not inherit. It will surprise my friends, however, to learn that I had as a boy an exceptionally good soprano voice. Once a week I received singing lessons from a Mr Breeze. He had a fine baritone voice, and his principal claims to fame were that in his younger days he sang with the great Galli-Curci, and his son was the well-known Alan Breeze, who to his father's undisguised horror was the vocalist in Billy Cotton's band.

Under Mr Breeze's tuition I won a medal at the Stratford Musical Festival, and I was in some demand to sing at concerts in aid of charity. In those days such concerts were held on Sundays at the London theatres, and I sang to crowded theatres at both the Hippodrome and the Palladium. The crowds, I need hardly add, came to hear and see the top-liners (who gave their services free) and not to hear me. There is no doubt, however, where I gave my finest performance. Mr Breeze entered my name for a competition organized by one of the daily newspapers. The venue was, of all places, in the basement of a department store called Beale's in the Holloway Road. I duly repaired there with my mother to sing, in Italian, Toselli's *Serenade*, whose words I had committed to memory phonetically under the guidance of Mr Breeze.

My turn duly came, and I stepped to the front of the stage to sing for the judges, each of whom, I am sure, was distinguished in the musical world. I must have been about twelve years of age, and while I was not generally nervous when singing, I found the competitive element rather overwhelming. About half-way through the piece my memory suddenly deserted me. I momentarily paused, to the evident dismay of the accompanist and the obvious concern of the judges. What, I thought, do I do now? I waited for the floor to open and dispose of my problem, but it did not move. I then continued with the song, making up words which I hoped might sound like Italian. 'Nelcho sprongodore, de sponcho amore,' I sang. I seemed to be getting by, when one of the judges began to smile, and then to laugh. This infectiously travelled through all the judges until they were all laughing, at which point I began to laugh with them. I could not sing another note, and did not win a prize.

RUTH RENDELL
Crime Novelist

My Grandmothers

he first thing which comes to mind when I remember my grandmothers is that one of them would let me play the piano and the other wouldn't. This has so coloured my memories of them that I am left, even now, with the impression that one was kind and tolerant and the other tyrannical.

At that time my parents had no piano, I couldn't play and all I wanted to do was strum away and make a din. My father's mother, who lived in Plymouth, on Mutley Plain, and whom we visited every year at Easter, used to let me play the piano in the front room whenever I liked. Or so I remember it. It may in fact only have happened once or twice. 6 Hillside Avenue was a small granite house with a narrow lane running along the back of it between granite walls from which grew festoons of ivy-leaved toadflax. To us, far away in London, it was always simply known as 'Hillside', just as my other grandparents' house was familiarly called 'A hundred and three.'

This was its number in Grove Hill, not far from where we lived. A double-fronted Victorian house of considerable size, it had no 'front room' as such but a dining room on one side of a large hall and a vast drawing room on the other and in there was the piano. Both my grandmothers were small thin women, handsome and white-haired. Whether my paternal grandmother was highly strung and twitchy I don't know – she died when I was ten – but my mother's mother suffered from her nerves. Her nerves, usually distinguished by the adjective 'poor', were invoked when I wanted to play the piano. They seemed to be principally centred in her ears, for it was always these which she covered with spread hands and arms akimbo-like when she mentioned them.

She was part Swedish, part Danish, and neither she nor my grandfather ever learned to speak English well. We called them Mormor (mother's mother) and Morfar (mother's father) according to the charming Scandinavian custom. My father's parents were Grandma and Grandad. So far as I know, my grandmothers never met. The distance from London to Plymouth seemed much greater then than it does now and I wonder what Grandma would have thought of my flying there as I did last year, in just under an hour from Heathrow. Anyway, my father's mother disapproved of his marrying a foreigner and wouldn't go to the wedding, though they all became more or less reconciled later on.

We used to eat high tea at 'Hillside', a meal that started with tinned pears or peaches and thin bread and butter and continued to the next course of an enormous tongue. I don't remember ever eating in this way elsewhere, especially with a tinned fruit starter. My two young aunts were very pretty and I suspect very lively. They had been brought up with great propriety and were not allowed to wear bare-backed dresses to dances. One of them kept a lipstick hidden in a crack in the woodwork inside the front door and used to apply it speedily just before she went out.

The hall at 'A hundred and three' was hung with tapestries which my mother and her sister said were Gobelins. It seems unlikely. They were mostly grey with hints of murky red and dark brown and I thought them hideous and frightening. I didn't like being left alone in the hall because the tapestries swayed a little and the figures on them and the trees and horses seemed to move of their own volition. Morfar had picked them up somewhere, just as he had picked up the four-poster bed with Sphinxes on the posts that was supposed to have belonged to the Empress Josephine, the great carved table (which I now possess) and the plaster casts of statuary which loomed all over the house.

One of my grandmothers called me by the first of my Christian names and the other by the second. This was allegedly because Mormor could not pronounce the letter R in the English way, but I suspect the true reason was that each chose the name *her* child had picked to bestow on me. Going to 'A hundred and three' was a chore and a penance, visiting 'Hillside' a joy to be looked forward to for weeks. Children are unfair and capricious in their judgements and now I think the very different feelings I had towards my grandmothers was mostly due to those pianos. How simple it is to build yourself a reputation that lasts half a century beyond your death! It may be founded on no more than two kind words and permission – or two cross words and forbiddance.

Michael Holroyd

David Hicks

The Rt Rev Dr George Carey
(front row, centre)

Victorian Aunts

have always had the impression that my father's family did not entirely approve of his choice of wife, which did not prevent their marriage being a happy success; I can remember being taken to my paternal grandmother's house many times, but Mum seemed never to be with us. Grandma lived in a comfortable house on the North Shore of Sydney at Roseville, an aptly if unimaginatively named suburb, for indeed roses seemed to thrive in that particular place. I remember that the street was not surfaced and a small stream ran where a gutter would be, so that each house had a tiny wooden bridge in front of the gate. Grandma lived in bed, cared for by Pop's three sisters who remained spinsters all their lives. It was a strangely religious Protestant family, rather genteel, and the house had an atmosphere certainly lacking in ours, where beer was drunk and bets placed on unreliable horses over the telephone to an S.P. (starting price) bookmaker (illegal). Although Pop loved and respected his sisters, I feel that he was glad to have escaped the family, with a long tradition of church sidesmen.

Grandma died quite soon, but I still used to visit my aunts. I liked them all; Gertrude had been a member of 'The Grey Battalion' of nursing sisters in the 1914–18 war and had seen much overseas service and had been decorated many times; Muriel was a tiny hunchback, a sweet lady, and Florence was the eldest with a warm straightbacked authority. They all clasped their hands over their stomach and all wore metal-rimmed glasses with little gold chains pinned to their blouses.

I do not recall any hard evidence as to why our branch of the family differed from the others except, as I have said, that Pop married a different sort of woman than was expected and preferred. It would have been said then that he had married beneath him, and I believe that it may have caused some estrangement, though not from his sisters. He was the youngest son of a family possessing the qualities of intelligence, industriousness, loyalty, honesty and respectability; I would swear that my aunts never lied, betrayed a trust, or were disrespectful to their parents. They reflected piety, love, warmth and humour, adult virtues from a Victorian childhood. I was too young to value them, and realize now that they were quite remarkable and lovely women.

Pop shared their virtues, except that of piety; I think he was a petted pony that kicked over the traces a bit, and Mum was the sort of girl his father may have called 'flighty'.

Our family fortunes went up and down through those difficult years between the wars like the popular yo-yo of that time. Pop, on the way up in a large company, was conspired against and lost a promising position; he was not a winner, either, for which I am ever grateful – he would not have been the beaut father he was, otherwise.

LOUIS BENJAMIN

President, Stoll Moss Theatres Ltd

The Strange Affair of the Chicken Soup

 refer to what I can only describe as 'The Strange Affair of the Chicken Soup'.

To give some background to this extremely long running event I would explain my early childhood. I was brought up in the then customary poor Jewish family. Mine was only an exception in the size and make up of it.

I had two older sisters, making the immediate circle five, and three maiden aunts (all sisters of my mother) which made a household of six females, and my father and myself. I am certain that this influenced my attitude towards women to this very day. Whilst not being chauvinistic I tend to feel, most of the time, somewhat impervious to the female viewpoint, bearing in mind that I, in turn, have two daughters. My Aunts Annie and Birdie both went to work, whilst Aunt Esther remained to help my mother with domestic chores which included cooking, shopping and laundering the entire family's wardrobe in a tin bath.

Chicken Soup arrived at least once a week, normally at lunchtime on Saturday and it was made in the following manner. You purchased a boiling chicken, which was I believe a penny cheaper than a roasting chicken; the soup was made with the chicken whole and at a given moment it was taken out and placed in the oven to roast. This resulted in a two course meal for eight people for a penny less than a one course meal.

Following my years living at home I spent a short time in digs in Liverpool, whilst working there as an Assistant Manager. I was then called up to the Army for the next three and a half years, which I spent mostly in India and Burma. The cuisine in these places gave me no reason to alter my views on soup. This changed in 1954 when my newly wedded wife cooked her first meal in our furnished flat in Morecambe, Lancashire. Fate decreed that it had to be roast chicken. When she provided it I asked the logical question, 'where's the soup?' – only to find, to my horror, that she had bought a roasting chicken and had put it directly into the oven.

I honestly believed, at that moment, that I had made a dreadful mistake and married a spendthrift. The conclusion, however, to the story is that she now makes me chicken soup, the only difference is that today she leaves the chicken in it. Which only goes to show what a little money and a modicum of success can do to one's standard of living.

BOBBY BALL
Comedian

Inherited Memories

When I was a child, my family were very poor, but one of my fondest memories is when my father was working nights.

Me and my two sisters used to crawl into the big double bed with my mother and would sleep top to toe after talking long into the night. I would be at the bottom of the bed with my middle sister, and my eldest sister and mother would be at the top. My mother used to talk to us about when she was a young lady and also tell us *her* childhood memories. We were all snuggled down together and I've never forgotten the lovely feeling to this day.

These are *my* childhood memories.

THE HON SIR ANGUS OGILVY KCVO

Director of Sothebys

An Afternoon With Peter Pan

y childhood was spent at our home in Scotland. I am full of many happy memories – but there is one particular afternoon which I have never forgotten.

One Sunday when I was very young, my godfather came to lunch with my parents. Afterwards he took me off alone for a long walk in the woods nearby. During the course of that afternoon he told me in graphic detail all about a young friend of his who lived there. His name was Peter Pan. On subsequent occasions whenever I visited those woods I was absolutely certain that sooner or later I would run into Peter Pan – but, of course, I never did.

What in fact had happened was that I was lucky enough – at a very impressionable age – to meet the author and the creator of Peter Pan. My delightful godfather, you see, was Sir James Barrie.

That magical afternoon occurred well over fifty years ago – but I still remember it as vividly as if it all happened only yesterday. What a truly wonderful present to be able to give to one's godchild – a memory which has never faded.

SIR PETER IMBERT QPM
Commissioner of Police of the Metropolis

Clutches of the Law

learest memories, it seems, are often those which don't do one much credit. Even as a very young boy, I recall incidents which indicated that I had a keen sense of justice, albeit my judgement was often clouded by childish illogicalities. The start of my school life coincided with the outbreak of the Second World War, for which I claim no responsibility! An important part of the war effort was the campaign to utilize every bit of space to grow vegetables. As children we didn't really understand that food could no longer be shipped to this country. U-boats sinking our food ships was not a reality to us but we were nonetheless caught up in the enthusiasm for allotments and home food production. My primary school was no exception and I remember the pride I had in a sixth share of a plot in the school gardens. My particular part was well tended and nestling near to what I thought was one of the largest oak trees in Kent. Beyond that was a small wilderness which often provided labour for those of us who had not exactly pleased the gardening master, Mr Harris – a giant of a man who had recently retired from the Metropolitan Police.

For whatever reason about half a dozen of us were selected one morning – which coincided with our turn to tend our own plots – to clear the wilderness. The only attraction it had was that it was near the pig-sties which always fascinated me; but we were affronted to see that others, who only the day before had worked on their own plots, were again the favoured few. At nine or ten years of age my intense feeling of injustice was not matched by an ability to articulate the grievances of our small band of urchins, nor by common sense. The sequence of events is dimmed by the passage of time, but having been singled out by Mr Harris as the troublemaker – and neither he nor I could have had any inkling that I might one day follow him into the Metropolitan Police Service – I recall him bearing down on me and the rest of my group like a charging rhinoceros. That particular moment of apprehension I shall always remember most clearly. His large wellington boots probably slowed him down a bit, but what I recall as a 6'6" giant was almost upon me. Reason was not one of my boyhood attributes and I took to my heels and ran, life was precious and the war

112

in Europe and the Far East seemed suddenly to have much less significance than my flight from this Goliath. I dodged around one side of the great oak, over the gardens but my way out of the gardens was barred by a diminutive, and I seem to recall a pretty, but stern teacher Mrs Forman – the wife of our local policeman no less – who was taking a girls' physical education class on the lawn.

Life seemed to be closing in as I heard the roar of Mr Harris closing the gap behind me, and I saw too that he was carrying a large garden spade. There was no thought of the consequences as I hurled the nearest bit of ammunition at him; whether it was a clod of hard earth or a newly dug swede I can't remember. My accuracy must have been sharpened by the panic I was in, as he parried the object with a defensive stroke, which would not have shamed the great Kent cricketer Leslie Ames. This delay enabled me to skip round Mrs Forman, over the garden wall, across the playground and out of the school gates. It must have been three hours after the end of the school day that I dared go home; sitting first in a rockery behind the cemetery and then hidden amongst the piles of wood in a local timber yard, the full horror of what I had done and my predicament dawned on me. There was no sympathy at home and the next morning saw me standing as the accused urchin, in the playground outside the headmaster's study, the class lined up to witness my discomfiture as I apologized.

To my surprise Mr Harris, who turned out to be a very gentle giant, chose me to work on my plot that morning. I little deserved it but somehow his humanity rubbed salt into my wounded feelings but I had learned a very harsh but valuable and long-lasting lesson. I seem to have been in the clutches of the police ever since.

Crackling from the Sky

recall the tremendous change that the outbreak of the war made to our school arrangements. At first there were no air raid shelters available at school and we had to go in small groups for lessons at the homes of our teachers. To see our teachers in their home environment was an interesting and novel experience. One of the teachers to whose home I went had a small terrier. I fear that I remember more of his somewhat threatening aspect towards my ankles than I remember of the lessons we were then being taught.

When air raid shelters had been built we returned to school but in two shifts since the shelters could only accommodate half of the pupils at any one time and so we had a long succession of half days, either in the morning or the afternoon. The need for these arrangements was emphasised as I crossed an open park – called Bruntsfield Links – one afternoon. It was a beautiful clear afternoon. I heard crackling from the sky and I saw a large aeroplane being pursued, as it seemed, by much smaller planes and white lines coming from the wings of the smaller planes directed towards the larger. It could not be an air raid – the air raid warning had not sounded – but it was – the first German air raid on our islands – an attack on the Forth Railway Bridge, near Edinburgh, in which no hits were scored on the Bridge and all the attacking bombers were crippled.

Chairman Marlborough Fine Art Ltd

The School Result

 was brought up in Cornwall in a very out-of-the-way place. Consequently before going to school, which I did at the age of nine and three-quarters, I had received virtually no education and was unable to read, partly due to the fact that indulgent grown-ups seemed prepared to read to me, convincing me that the ability to do so was unnecessary.

However, the terrible day came when, on arrival at my private school, the custom was for everyone to undergo a form of elementary exam to find out which form they should be placed in and then, on the first Saturday, the whole school was called together to hear the results.

When my name was called, the headmaster announced in a terrifying voice that an extraordinary thing had happened. The most ignorant boy in the history of the school was in their midst. All eyes turned on me and I was set upon as if by a pack of hounds.

Being, no doubt, an insensitive boy, I was not unduly upset by this, but merely surprised by the unpleasant side of boys in a mob to which I had not previously been subjected.

I would like to be able to say that I went on to achieve incredible scholastic achievements but can only report that my progress subsequently was average.

MARTYN LEWIS
Television newsreader

A Tale of Two Schools

My parents were Welsh and I was born in Swansea, but when I was six we moved to Portrush in Northern Ireland. My co-ed school, Dalriada, was a forty minute bus ride away in Ballymoney. It was a long way to go at first – at the age of six – but I loved it.

After the 11-plus my parents moved me to an all-boys' school nearby, but I was very unhappy there. I was an extremely fat lad and was picked upon and involved in a lot of fighting. Because of this, I developed a stutter which lasted until my parents moved me back to my old school a year later, and then it disappeared completely in a few weeks.

I still have one small combination of words that gives me trouble but at least I can re-write them when I am reading the news.

I was reasonably extrovert as a child and my parents encouraged me to enter singing competitions and to do a lot of drama. Dalriada School was well-known for its Shakespeare and my first stage appearance at seven was playing an urchin boy in *The Merchant of Venice*. I adored acting and when I was ten took part in some BBC radio plays. Later I did a lot of public debating and edited the school magazine. It was all good practice for the work I finally chose to do.

THE RT HON THE LORD FRASER OF CARMYLLIE PC

The Lord Advocate

Journeys in Africa

ith a responsibility today that requires ceaseless dull movement between London and Edinburgh travelling has few attractions. For a ten-year-old schoolboy six train journeys a year of five nights and four days from the Congo border to the Cape Province were glorious, anarchic, dangerous and grubby.

Bravely smiling glistening-eyed mummies saw us off late at night spot-lessly clean, clutching carefully chosen healthy 'extras' for the journey. On the platform avoiding their anxious embraces was critical if the real task in hand was to be accomplished — lifting half-crowns and ten-bob notes off fathers and uncles so desperate to avoid any exchange revealing emotion that they paid up without a word.

On departure, six to a compartment, the financial success of the platform party was quickly reckoned up and the healthy food despatched out into the African night with only the orange peel carefully retained as ammunition for later corridor battles with catapults. Bunks were fought over with priority accorded for un-mentionable reasons to the upper ones. And then late into the next morning after little understood and loosely governed games of pontoon some sleep.

The next day was spent planning for the Victoria Falls that evening. For the audacious and affluent that meant hiring a taxi from Livingstone, sneaking in a swim at the posh Victoria Falls Hotel and, with luck, rejoining the train across the border. For the less adventurous Livingstone Station was scoured for rocks to heave over the bridge in to the Zambesi Gorge from the open balconies on each carriage. A truly pointless exercise: even if the bridge was cleared no rock could ever be seen to hit the water hundreds of feet below.

After changing trains at Bulawayo and meeting up with new clean recruits the routine for the next three days was quickly established; no regular meals only biltong and Coke; little changing of clothes and certainly no washing; endless arguments and fights with any mention of school or parents off limits. There were lunatic games swinging from bunk straps outside the carriage from one compartment to another and under no circumstances was any word to be exchanged with a sister or any other girl travelling more sensibly under supervision.

The last afternoon climbing up to Grahamstown with a second locomotive at the rear brought about a sharp change of mood. The only clean shirt was donned in a useless attempt to conceal from an unsmiling school matron the grime and stains of the journey. The contraband and vicious weaponry expensively acquired in Mafeking, Kimberley or Bloemfontein was invariably discovered and confiscated. An adult world restored forgotten standards and exacted stern punishment. Still it had been heady freedom never experienced now in a Shuttle lounge.

ROBERT N. WOODWARD

Founder and Honorary Chairman, CLIC Trust

Escapes and Escapades

The idea of being evacuated seemed very remote, although it had been mentioned so many times at my school, Dr Bells in Fishponds, Bristol, because my older brothers, John and David, were also to be evacuated with me. It had been impressed upon us by our head-master, Mr Cook, that a great deal of extra organization had to go into the sending away of three boys from the same family. My youngest brother, Alan, was to 'escape' as he was only three and could therefore stay at home.

I still remember some of the conversations at home and the unhappy look on my mother's face when we discussed the plans for our departure. Whilst talking with some of my school chums, there seemed to be an element of adventure in the whole exercise, but there was also a feeling in the pit of my stomach that made me feel quite sick at the thought of leaving home. I wondered what would happen in the air raids when in the past we had all been ushered downstairs and I slept on the wide shelf in the cupboard under the stairs. Or some times we would go across to Wendover School and stay with other families in the cellar until the siren was sounded for the 'all-clear'.

I cannot remember the date, but I shall never forget the Saturday morning when John, David and I picked up our battered cases and the cardboard boxes which contained our gas masks. After saying cheerio to my father, mother took the three of us on the long walk from our home to Alexandra Park School in Fishponds to join the other children ready for the departure in two coaches bound for Taunton. The awful feeling of separation as we turned the corner in the coach was almost too much to bear, and the journey seemed to take a life-time. We arrived at a village just outside the town where we were taken into the village hall for buns and cups of tea. On our arrival we each had labels tied to the strings that held our gas mask boxes and someone with a large register was pairing the various children off with the local people who had offered to open their homes and extend their families for the duration of the war.

Difficulties began to arise when first John was paired with David and I was left out. Then John and I were paired and David began to howl, and then David and I were put together and John broke down. It became very clear after five or ten minutes that there was no way anyone could split the three brothers, and a very courageous couple named Saunders agreed to take all three of us but pointed out that their spare room had only two single beds and we would have to make the best of it.

This particular upset behind us, we travelled with the Saunders to the little bungalow which I think was on the Trull road going out of Taunton. We made a dash for home on the Saturday night because we saw flashes in the sky and we were afraid our home was being bombed. We were 'recaptured' and Mr Saunders, who I think must have had a small haulage business, took us out for a ride in his lorry on Sunday to try and settle us down. Flashes in the sky on the Sunday night resulted in us making another dash for home, to be rounded up by a very patient Mr and Mrs Saunders. Again, in an effort to help us to settle, Mr Saunders said that we should have a few days off school and help him deliver some wood during the course of the week. We had a great time on the Monday morning delivering the wood, only to find that some miserable kid next door, whose surname I think was Hughes, had brought a letter from his headmaster at the local school to Mr and Mrs Saunders, as a result of him reporting us for not attending school. And so we went to school after lunch on Monday, and I suspect young Master Hughes will still remember his good hiding on Monday evening!

The rest of the week continued in much the same way and on the Friday Mr and Mrs Saunders told us that they had spoken to the headmasters in Taunton and in Bristol and had got a message to our parents, and they were all agreed that we could return home on Saturday for good. We were beside ourselves with the sheer joy of going home and I had a feeling that Mr and Mrs Saunders felt that to a large extent the war was over when we left!

Mr Cook met us at Temple Meads Station and he and Mr Harry Herbert, our form teacher, were obviously very angry and we were told we must all report first thing on Monday morning to be disciplined for the huge amount of trouble we had caused in such a short time. The threat of punishment in no way detracted from the pleasure in knowing we were home.

When we arrived at home father gave us quite a ticking-off, but I could tell from the look on his face that the reprimand was quite different from usual and he really was not annoyed at all. Mother certainly did not tell us off, and I had the feeling that she was as thrilled as we were to be back together as a family.